SPACE AND MY LIFE

(A Layman's Choice of Understanding)

SPACE AND MY LIFE

(A Layman's Choice of Understanding)

SAMIR KANTI

PARTRIDGE
A Penguin Random House Company

To order additional copies of this book, contact
Partridge India
000 800 10062 62
orders.india@partridgepublishing.com

www.partridgepublishing.com/india

This book is dedicated to the memory of my father, Pradyota Kumar Sarkar, mother, Juthika Rani Sarkar, my father-in-law, Haraprasad Aich and mother-in-law, Namita Aich. In those hard days of our shifting to West Bengal from our sweet home in present Bangla Desh as displaced persons, my parents took all the hardships in keeping their children safe and sound. Because of my parents and parents-in-law mentally I could come close to Sadhu Baba and Thakur Baba, the two enlightened saints.

Thanks to my wife Dipti Sarkar, my daughter Ruchira, son Shuvadeep and daughter-in-law Minakshi and my grandson Shayan (son of Ruchira) in encouraging me to write this book. While writing this book, we were blessed with a sweet angel (daughter of Shuvadeep and Minakshi – name not decided yet).

Space and My Life

(A Layman's Choice of Understanding)

MY FRIENDS,

SPACE is a 5-letter word. But its significance is infinite. There is Universal Space, or, rather endless Space beyond the known/imagined Universe. By logic we are to agree that this Space is stable and never ending (to be discussed later on). The expanding Universe occupies a part. Even then it could not wholly occupy that part. Most of the area remains void of matters. Even in the tiny articles of atoms and molecules, most of the spaces remain void. Imagine, there is nothing absolutely solid. Even in a solid iron rod, there will be millions of spaces and super energy can pass through it.

And there is Space in our mind – thinking and dreaming, travelling endless Space. And there is Space in our mind for accommodation of desires of different natures, good or bad, positive or negative. When we say, he is optimistic, or, he is pessimistic, does it also hold some space of our mind? May be. Because, it depends on Hope and Patience. How much space they occupy in your mind, it matters. A long rope of patience gives strength to hope, even though the present might be under bad conditions. Same thing is for Faith. It is not ruled by Logic. We say, he places faith to everyone and thus he suffers in many occasions. We cannot explain why it is so with that someone. It largely depends on the basic nature of qualities occupying the space of our mind. All these qualities cannot be explained by DNA. I think, keeping the basic structure intact for one's DNA, some changes may come through the course of one's life, being influenced by the mind set and by the basic character of the job where one is engaged. I believe the job of a priest and that of a trader in butchering the chickens and selling the meat will have different impacts on mind and on their DNA. Their mental and physical reactions to any identical situation would be different.

Space: its contribution to human life is immense. If you think of it, you would feel it at every moment of your life. Not the cosmic Space, but the Space exercising by you, or, being experienced by you in your everyday life.

How much space you allow, or, inclined to allow in your life, for different human qualities, good and bad, are very important to steer your sailing in this life and also in your life beyond this mortal state of life in flesh and bones on this planet.

Let me be a little more expressive. You would find that there are many boys and girls who have shown their keenness in achieving some higher position either as a Sportsman, or, as Engineer/Doctor/Scientist/Academician etc. And because of their zeal, they automatically give a high space of their mind to their "Will". And, poor or rich, they attain their goal which is recognized by others.

And there are many sufferers in late life for giving "Ample Space" in their mind for doing wrong jobs in trying short cut ways to be prominent figures, either financially, or, socially, or, politically. After achieving the goal they become happy, no doubt, but always with nightmares for being under trial one day, or, for being punished by someone used by him to climb up the ladder. And for many of them, a day comes, when they get ditched in gutters, either prisoned or killed or losing their fame and money in womanizing, gambling etc.(because, these qualities quickly come in the atmosphere of wrong doings). Nobody can be totally good or totally bad. Your action depends on how much space of your mind is occupied by good instincts and how much by bad instincts. With more of good instincts, the bad instincts would remain dormant, as good instincts would not allow them to come up. If your dream is to be reached and at the same time your space in mind is full of good instincts, you cannot take bad measures in fulfilling your dream. You would take the hard path of labor with honesty and sincerity in achieving the goal. It may not come as per your expectations, but you will not be disheartened. Such is the power of working honestly.

Then there is the question of enjoying life. Here also much depends on the spaces occupied by positive and negative forces in your mind. To enjoy life, it does not depend much whether you are poor or rich. It definitely depends whether you are leading a normal healthy life, or, miserably sick, which again mostly governed by the way you are passing your daily life. Of course, some are born with misfortunes, physically handicapped. Even some of them, with mind's space filled with the positive forces like courage, hope, zeal and patience, do well in overcoming their sorrows and difficulties.

In my life, I have felt the touch of Almighty in several occasions, to give me courage to overcome extreme bad conditions. This was because I allowed ample space in my mind for faith in existence of God and for the faith that if you pray, he would respond. Many times I have narrowly escaped the danger of being hurt physically and many times I have been able to come out of difficult situations, as if someone is watching me and extending the helping hand to protect me. My service life was full of adventures right from the very first year, when I was 24 years old and up to the age of 66, when I was working in the deep forests of Democratic Republic of Congo (DRC).

Not only that. In rare two/three occasions it has happened that I felt the desire to taste some sweets or fruits. The items were not in the house. So, the best way is to forget it. Lo! Some relation paid an unexpected visit carrying that *something I desired. Is it accidental? Is it just coincidence? Or, it is the soft touch of someone looking after us. With these small incidences your faith grows, occupying your mind.*

It must have happened with you also. Whether you notice it, or, overlook it, depends much on the Faith occupying the space of your mind. We have become man with so much capacity in thinking, completely different from any other member of the Plant and Animal Kingdom. Many scientists would say, this is just an accidental event in the history of life on earth. But others would say, it is a planned way of evolution, first from unicell to multicell, simple body system to complex and more complex body system and simple brain to more complex brain, like simple computer to more complex computer, as if, someone has coded the Plan to play a Big and Most Versatile Game. In this way, the space between the tiny structural elements as that of atoms and molecules, the space between the celestial bodies, the space in the known Universe and beyond, the space in our mind, all become linked and related. You can say, the space of mind is abstract. The cosmic space or, the Mother Space is also abstract. Can you imagine the never ending space? Endless Space! You cannot imagine, but logically you are to believe it. This we would discuss later on.

Sometime, the circumstances abruptly bring changes in the space in your life. If it is good for you, it is nice. But, if it is bad, bringing uncertainty in the smooth flow of your life, have patience and courage to accept it and then to fight to modify the bad space. Gradually, with your efforts and zeal, the space around you would change in your favor. The life history of everybody on the Earth teaches many lessons how to go about life on earth, keeping faith in self and in God and having patience to endure the bad situation and try honestly and sincerely to come out of it.

You would get courage, if you place faith in God and depends on his love and mercy for you. This would give you ample hope and patience to overcome the bad stretches of life. You would not think of ending your life, or, asking for death. This depends on how much space in your mind you are keeping for God. It should not be just a ritual, but love, faith and affection to God.

There was a topsy-turvy change in our life after Independence of India through partition of Bengal. It was 1940s. We were *a family of 08 persons (parents Pradyota Kumar Sarkar and Juthika Sarkar, 04 elder sisters, Dipti, Tripti, Preeti and Smriti and we two brothers, Samir and Mihir), living in a remote village Kotakole in Lohagara subdivision under the Jessore district of Bengal (present Bangla Desh) in British India. My maternal uncle's place was Bagerhat, close to Khulna. My maternal grandfather, Jatindra Nath Basu, was Headmaster-in-Charge of Bagerhat High School (that time it was not called higher secondary school). In 1940s and 1950s, the education system was up to class X in school, followed by 02 years in Intermediate (I.A./I.SC./I.Com), 02 years in Under-Graduation(B.A./B.Sc./B.Com) and 02 years in Post-graduation (M.A./M. Sc./M.Com).*

I was born in Bagerhat under the care of our maternal grandmother Chapala Basu on 3rd January, 1941. That much space of comfort was with us that for any problem, or, need, we could take shelter in "Mamabadi" (house of maternal uncle). In Kotakole, there was no hospital, no village health center, and no doctor practicing privately. But it was a village where we felt comfortable among our close and distant relations from own side and a few from in-law's side of some family members. The other inhabitants were our

"Praja" (as the term was in use), i.e., the farmers who used to cultivate our land, divided in small and large plots among the relations. That was the comfortable Space – Time endeavor for us.

There was ample space in life for 'go easy' living, if you do not care for not having any medical facilities nearby. Yes, the medical facilities were available in Khulna – a distance of 41km. In remote places, not connected by motor able roads and not having any transport facilities except bullock carts and boats, distance in kilometer has no meaning. It should be time – distance, like the celestial distances, measured in time taken by light to reach the place. In our case, it should be measured in time taken by journey by foot/palki (palanquin)/bullock cart to Madhumati river ghat (area prepared to go down the slope/stair to the water front) and then by boat through Madhumati and Rupsa rivers to Khulna.

Easy going life. There was no urge in any body's mind to see that the children are brought up to face comfortably higher competitions in getting higher technical education to be engineer/doctor/academicians etc.

But the situation was different for Bagerhat, especially for my maternal uncles, *their father (my maternal grandfather) Jatindra Nath Basu being the renowned headmaster of Bagerhat School.*

I still remember many events of my stay in Kotakole. These are now soothing memories, like rowing a boat at the age of 6 starting from our pond to the canal to 'bil' (vast stretch of water) during the rainy season, when the river Madhumati used to overflow the banks and flowing through the paddy fields, surrounding the high land of the village establishments. Our pond, the low level tracks around the village and the vast stretches of paddy field – all became part and parcel of the vast stretch of water body. The only way to go from one village to the other village was by boat. The result of rowing boat at that age was that three times I fell in the water. Unlike a village boy, I did not know swimming at age 6. Once I was saved by my distant uncle's mother (Thakuma) whom I was taking by boat to the opposite bank of the pond, only a small stretch remaining above water. While approaching the bank I gave a last push to the boat. I did not notice that the boat was heading towards a strong banana plant. It dashed against the plant and I simply fell in the water. The second time I fell in water in a peculiar way. I used to notice that the seniors used to place the right foot on the boat and then by giving a push to the land by the left foot used to go quickly inside the pond. One day in the noon hour, I tried it. I placed the right foot on the boat and then gave a push to the land by the second foot. It did not come to my mind to immediately take up my second foot from the land. As a result my legs stretched with the moving boat and I fell in the water. There were people taking bath in the pond. They rescued me. I do not remember how I fell in the third time and who rescued me. One thing I should mention here. Before these incidents, once when we were coming from 'Mamabadi', a lady saint (we called her Guruma; she was a disciple of Shri Shri Dhyananda Swami) cautioned my father that I had the 'phara' (destiny for an accident) of drowning in water. She suggested for worshipping Mother Ganga (goddess) in a river. After these incidents, my father took me by a boat to the river Madhumati and I performed the worship. In summer and winter, the situation was different. This vast stretch of water body vanished, except the water in the ponds.

One event I like to narrate as a lesson for the guardians to small kids. I was 06 years old. In every afternoon my charge used to be given to a servant Mainuddin who used to take me to strides through the village, sometime through the farming land. I guess, his age was around 20. Once he asked me how the children are born. I said,' they come from heaven. My mother has told me that I have come from heaven'. He said, 'You have been fooled. They come from the womb of women. 'How'? Then he narrated in details the act which is responsible for producing the children and told me, 'I would show you one night. Our house walls are made of jute sticks (patkati). I have seen through the openings between the sticks this act of my elder brother with boudi (brother's wife). Then discussing with my married friends, I learnt how to do it.' This is the first time I learnt what is called sex.

So, I ate the Adam's apple. And that put a blow on my divine innocence as a child. I am not against sex education, but not at this age, killing the divine innocence. My advice: never allow your children to be alone with young servants – both boys and girls.

Perhaps, our future would be built up through our 'Mamabadi'. But there was a different plan by God, creating an unexpected Time – Space environment for us. The British Rule was over and two countries, India and Pakistan, were born out of undivided India on the 15th of

August, 1947 (the day when my 'would be' wife Dipti was born in Burdwan in Independent India). It was a pathetic and unfortunate decision of the political leaders. The Space – Time relation of our independence was not proper. The history says:

Under the leadership of Mahatma Gandhi the Indians moved to get rid of the British Rule in India, forming Indian National Congress. The Hindus, the Muslims, the Sikhs, the Jains were under the banner of Indian National Congress. Later on a group of Muslim politicians, to look after the interests of the Muslims, formed a separate party under the name of the Muslim League. At first it was decided that the British Rule would hand over the power to the Indian leadership in a peaceful manner. But the Muslim League started demanding for a separate country for the Muslim-majority area, proposing for a Hindu-majority India and a Muslim-majority Pakistan. Indian National Congress was against this proposal of dividing India into two independent countries. The Muslim League called for a general strike on the 16th of August, 1946 under the banner of Direct Action Day. This resulted to a severe riot between the Hindus/Sikhs and the Muslims. The worst sufferers were Calcutta and Noakhali of Bengal, Lahore of Punjab, the North-Western Frontier Province, followed by some places of United Province (present Uttar Pradesh) and Bihar. In three days of riot in Calcutta four thousand people died and around one lakh people became homeless. This is notoriously known as the Great Calcutta Killings. The Noakhali riot was also very severe, involving mass killings, rapes, tortures, looting of movable properties from the houses and shops of the Hindus and burning their houses. This is known as the Noakhali Genocide.

However, after this noble act of the politicians, the Space of living in the life of common people widely changed, through partition of Bengal on the eastern front and partition of Punjab on the western front, followed by the conflicting issue of Kashmir who joined India under the opposition of Pakistan – a problem solely arose because of the division of our country into India and Pakistan. Ah! Like Berlin, if we could join together again, may be against the Will of Politicians of both the countries; but for their evil presence, we could settle comfortably in one country of Hindus, Muslims, Sikhs, Christians, Persians, Tribals and other sects of undivided British India.

A second division in people's living came, when Pakistan occupied a part of Kashmir by force, thereby practically dividing Kashmir into East Kashmir and West Kashmir, or, Pakistan Occupied Kashmir (POK).

Within a few years of Independence, how the Space in Human Life changed in this part of the World! Riot and partition embossed an unprecedented hatred in the mind of Hindus and Muslims. Even to-day, 68 years after partition, we are getting hatred lessons for each other and we are facing physical and mental hazards through the so called extremists.

See the life of the so called extremists in action. Most of them were poor, poorly educated and were easy prey to be mobilized by money power and brain washing lessons in the name of religion from a good number of cunning and no-ethics people for their personal welfare – collection of funds from many fools who think that it is a pious activity in the name of religion to bring sorrows and distress to the people of other religions. They do not understand that the All mighty is One and only One and we all are His dear ones.

They are also getting fat funds from the countries who try to dominate over their neighbors by creating internal disturbances within the neighboring countries. And some countries feel happy to create conflict between the other countries so that they can sell warheads to them, like bombers and fighter planes, transport helicopters and vehicles, arms and ammunitions. These all happen, because the Space in living is quite different between the Developed, Developing and Poor Countries. It is not only a space difference in living, but a Space difference in thinking which gradually built up after hundreds of years of different ways of living. With materialistic civilization man becomes more and more selfish.

Nobody thinks of giving Space in action, i.e. Patience. Patient hearing is important not only in between family members, but also between larger families of the World – the Countries. When men gathered the knowledge of cultivation, they started settling in convenient spaces, which gradually through hundreds of years of living turned into separate countries. A larger role of Space started – space in relation between family members, between Society members and between member countries. Everywhere is Space – Time trends. How it moves! Is it really in the hands of people? Or, is it destined? Dinosaurs got accustomed in a Space – Time environment and they could not survive through sudden change in the Space – Time environ.

Space. What is it? Is it 3-dimension occupied by your body, or, a 4-dimension by your body in a particular time? All events are in 4-dimension Spaces.

Coming to our story, in our village Kotakole, away from cities and towns, riot did not make any effect. Hindus and Muslims of our villages and the neighboring villages looked after each other as brothers and sisters. Our Muslim farmers and Muslim land owners came for our protection, to see that no outsider comes to kill us, or, to try to make a clash between the two sects.

While our family was making arrangements to leave the generation old dwelling units along with farming lands, cattle farms, ponds full of fish and mango orchards, leaving hundreds of years of legacy behind, the Muslim brothers came forward to request us not to go out. 'We would live together, as we were living for hundreds of years'.

Rumors started coming that there were infiltrations in some villages, disturbing the age old eco-system. Ultimately in 1948 our parents decided to leave for West Bengal. By the time our maternal uncles came to Krishna Nagar, the headquarters of the Nadia district. My father came there along with myself and my brother, 07 years and 04 years old and got a job in the Metropolitan Insurance Company (MIC). Actually my father and my eldest maternal uncle joined MIC earlier. With promotions, by 1948 my uncle had the charge of Nadia district unit of MIC. But my father left the job after working for two to three years. He did not like to continue in any town, leaving the grand way of living in an easy going life in Kotakole - farming lands, five mango orchards, tank full of fish, cows for milk, ducks for eggs, goats for meat and birds for shooting for extra dishes at time. And there were so many workers to obey his orders as a Landlord.

My four elder sisters were just studying at home under a village teacher. In 1948, they attained the age of 19, 17, 15 and 13. And we two brothers, 7 and 4, used to be taught by father and the elder sisters. The simple idea was that with this education, singing and cooking qualities, my parents would be able to find good matches for them in close-by villages, or, in Khulna/ Narail/Bagerhat/Jessore, where the relations are there to assist in matrimonial tie-ups. We had the relations from the in-law's side of my father in Calcutta also. Even my own grandfather had a timber shop-cum-go down in Maniktala in Calcutta. But most of the time he used to be in the village. The Manager took the advantage and the business drastically failed, my grandfather losing lot of money. He died, when my father was 07 years old. My father did well in the studies up to Intermediate (present Class XII Board Exam), but after that he could not continue the studies because of financial problems. He was very hard working and intelligent. He came out of that bad financial stage. Then at age of 44, in 1948, he faced the second blow to leave his entire property of Kotakole and to try for his luck in West Bengal. He had substantial property, but not much cash at hand. Substantial cash remained blocked in his business of making large transport boats.

Coming to the sisters' education at home, this was the system at that time in most of the villages. Higher education for girls was not an important thought in the mind of the parents. For the sons, well, my parents thought to shift us to Bagerhat, where our maternal grandfather Jatindra Nath Basu was the Headmaster (in-charge) of Bagerhat High School. And the direct admission to class IV or V was good enough – that was the thought.

But the 4-dimensional Space-Time relation changed abruptly for us – the Hindu habitats of East Bengal. In 1947 itself my eldest sister Dipti got married in a family in Khulna. In 1948, as mentioned earlier, our father brought us, the two brothers Samir and Mihir, in maternal uncle's place in Krishna Nagar. Father got a job in Metropolitan Insurance Company (MIC).

We were worried for our mother, living with three sisters in Kotakole. After six months, my father was posted to Ranaghat, opening an MIC branch there, based partly on salary and partly on commission, for promoting Life Insurance Policies. We felt it a great happy moment in our life, when my mother Juthika along with three sisters, Tripti, Preeti and Smriti joined us in a 2-bedroom rented house without any separate kitchen. The bathroom and toilet were shared with the landlord. Though we left our spacious house along with outer and inner courtyards in Kotakole, we enjoyed our stay in this small accommodation, as all the family members were together. But there was a pricking anxiety for our eldest sister Dipti, living in Khulna. However, after a year, in 1949 they could shift to Calcutta in a small house in Kalighat.

Then started a long period of patience and hard work for all of us, especially for my father in Ranaghat and for my only brother-in-law Rathindra Nath Basu in Calcutta in order to arrange for a decent modest living and education for the demanding members – my three unmarried sisters and for us, the two brothers. In 1949, our second sister Tripti, 18 years, felt that she was too old to get admission in a proper class in a school. She could read and write in Bengali and to some extent in English, along with a preliminary mathematical knowledge. Our third sister Preeti, 16 years, did not agree for this easy going life (thank God). She made a hard effort for getting education at home by a competent teacher and next year, in 1950, she was admitted in class VIII in a school for girls in Ranaghat. Hats off to her. In 1954 she was admitted in B.A. Courses in Krishna Nagar Government College. She was able to be graduated in 1956 and later on she became a teacher in a Government School in Budge Budge, close to Calcutta (in 1958 we shifted to Calcutta). She retired at the age of 60 and she is getting pension, living now along with her husband (retired from Central Excise services) and a son (in business) in their own house in Parnashree in Calcutta. Their daughter Mou is a Sr. Lecturer in Geology in Yogmaya Devi College in Calcutta. Her husband is in an MNC in Calcutta.

Our fourth sister, Smriti, 14 years in 1949, got admitted in a school in 1953 in class VII in Ranaghat. I was admitted in class III in 1950 at the age of 9. My brother Mihir got admitted in class III in 1953 at the age of 9. Smriti's effort in education was also not easy. In 1954 we came to Krishna Nagar on transfer of my father. For one year she was out of touch to any school. In 1955, however, she was admitted in class IX. Thanks to the teaching efforts put by our maternal grandfather in making her ready for admission in class IX. She also gave a lot of efforts in clearing the admission test. In 1956 she was matriculated (that time class X final examination was called matriculation).

After passing Intermediate, Smriti got a job of Telephone Operator in Telephone Exchange in Dalhousie in Calcutta. She was happy to continue the job till her retirement as Monitor on 31st December,

2000 at the recorded age of 60. She managed to lower her age on papers; otherwise she would not be considered to get the job in Telephone Exchange. This may be looked as bad, but at that Space of our life, we had to follow Darwin's theory of "Survival of the Fittest". Though the age difference between my fourth sister and me was 6 years, we got matriculated in 1956 and 1957. I remember, my matriculation examination got deferred twice, as some question papers were out. Perhaps I got impatient due to these interruptions and could not keep pace with the preparations. As a result, my results were not good as expected by others (I used to hold 3rd position all along in my school classes). I secured total marks of 479 out of 800, the 1st Division being 480. However I got a lesson – 'Do not be impatient. Keep yourself cool'.

I was admitted in Krishna Nagar Government College in I. Sc. (a course of 02 years) in 1957. Ours was a pure science with physics, chemistry, mathematics and the optional subject biology. It was a co-education college. Ah! What a good time we felt. There were 06 girls in our class. Every one appeared to be good looking to us. Two more girls used to join in the mathematics class. They were beautiful with very handsome physique. We took interest in keeping good attendance in the classes. And there were extra efforts to secure good marks in the class examinations so that our heads remain high to them, because these girls were very serious about the studies. We were also keen in helping them by sharing notes with them for the periods of their absence in the class teachings. And the day any one of them approached one of us for any help, that boy's body language suddenly changed and we used to envy him. As if, they were not just our classmates, they were queens and we were their obeyed soldiers. I understand, life was extra-good for them. Now-a-days the relation between the boys and the girls is quite normal, but that was not the case in our time. Perhaps in a much restricted society at that time, young boys were sex-starved at the adolescent age. By sex-starved I do not mean the physical contacts, but having closeness, more mental than physical, with the opposite folk. Gossiping together – that also was not taken in a light mood by the seniors.

However, their presence made us, at least some of us, more attentive to the studies. As a result I secured 75% marks in I. Sc. Final which was treated in our time as quite good marks. I got chances in admission with Physics Honors in St.

Xavier's college and in MBBS courses in Calcutta Medical College. Because of our financial status, we hesitated for my admission in the Medical College. My youngest maternal uncle Chhotomama (chhoto means small and mama means maternal uncle) advised me to take Honors in Geology. That time there was some good scope in getting job in the geological services. I got admitted in B.Sc. with honors in Geology and physics and mathematics as pass courses in Ashutosh College under the University of Calcutta.

That time, the under graduation course in Geology Honors was in Presidency college and in Ashutosh college under Calcutta University and in the Department of Geology under Jadavpur University. I passed B.Sc. with Honors in Geology in 1961.

My father was to retire in 1965. There was a dilemma in the family whether I should go for higher education, or, to try for a job as a graduate. There was scope for recruitment as a Trainee for Traffic Sergeant and be absorbed there on successful completion of training of one year. Somehow I had no inclination for that. And I loved the subject Geology. I understood the mental pressure on my father. He came, almost bare hand, to West Bengal in 1948 and made great efforts to earn bread and butter for us. His health also broke down. But, somehow I was confident that after completing M.Sc. in Geology I would get a job. We discussed. And my father agreed.

My friend X (name not given) and I from Ashtutosh College were very close to 1st class marks in Geology Honors (1961). We decided to go to the Jadavpur University for post-graduation, if seats were available after accommodating their students. We met Dr. S. Deb, Head of the Department of Geology, Jadavpur University. After seeing our marks, he gave a date to us for enquiry regarding the availability of seats. For that date, we decided to meet at a particular place (not remembering the place) and from there we would go together to meet Prof. Deb. I waited for more than an hour, but X did not turn up. I decided to meet Dr. Deb and to know the possibility of our admission. I was told that two hours before X met him and received 02 admission forms for him and for another boy. I went to the admission office and found them. X told me, 'Sorry. We (X and Y) decided to be together in M.Sc.'. This is the first time I experienced some silly politics in life. Dr. Deb, of course, agreed to take me, but being disheartened by their behavior

I joined the M.Sc. Course of Geology in Science College under the University of Calcutta. Though there were 10 students in M.Sc. in Presidency College and 10 in Science College under the University of Calcutta, all the classes were being taken jointly in Presidency College by the Geology teachers of both Presidency and Science Colleges. We passed out the M.Sc. Examination in 1963. In 1964 onward, the Science College opened their own geology class rooms in the Science College branch on Ballygunj Circular Road.

In 1962 my brother Mihir passed out Pre-University (that time the education system changed to 11 years in school and 01 year in Pre-University before being eligible for under-graduation courses) and got admitted in B.Sc. with Honors in Geology in Ashutosh College. In 1963 he was selected for admission in the Medical Sciences. He asked for our opinion. We saw the Sun rising in the horizon. Our father would be retiring in 1965, but my education is completed and hope, I would get a job in near future. And one Geologist is enough in a house. So, the brother joined the MBBS courses in Nilratan Sarkar Medical College under the University of Calcutta.

I passed out in 1963, securing high 1st class in M.Sc. in Geology. Though I stood 5th in rank, I secured highest marks in M.Sc. Thesis (dissertation) and Prof. Aniruddha De of the Department of Geology, Science College tried for a research job for me under CSIR (Council of Scientific and Industrial Research) with the place of study in Science College, University of Calcutta, located on the Ballygunj Circular Road, under the guidance of Dr. De. I was in CSIR pay scale with Rs. 250/- as monthly pay and Rs. 10/- as yearly increment. That time the rent for an average 3-room flat (not 3BHK), close to a main road, was just Rs. 50. The salary of a Jr. Geologist in GSI (a class I post) was Rs.350 which is now Rs. 40,000.

So, my father got some mental relief. Then, through the UPSC (Union Public Service Commission) examination of 1964, I was selected for a post of Assistant Geologist in Geological Survey of India (GSI). The close relatives got disheartened that I could not rank for the next higher post of Jr. Geologist in GSI through the same examination, but with 02 more subjects. In fact, I was not very serious about the UPSC exam, as my dream was to join some University/College as a lecturer, so that I could continue my research. My mental faculty was inclined to research work. Now after selection through UPSC I was in a dilemma what to do, especially with advice of our family members to join GSI. I consulted Prof. Ajit Kumur Suha of Geology Department, Presidency College and others. Most of them advised me to join GSI, as the scope was much limited in colleges and universities, and that too only after doing Ph.D., which used to take not less than 4/5 years. They said from their experience that there were lots of politics in educational institutes. Being a small environment, one cannot avoid the political atmosphere of a college, or, the rough behavior of the immediate boss. In GSI there is scope of taking transfer from one unit to the other in order to avoid such unwanted situations, GSI having regional offices in all the state capitals with the Central Headquarters in Calcutta.

Some advised me to continue research under CSIR. I went to Delhi to meet CSIR authorities in order to understand the future of my job as a Research Assistant. I was rebuffed, 'You people have got a platform under CSIR and now want to know the future, the career. Have patience and continue the work'. Ultimately, not having the courage to continue research as a CSIR Jr. Research Assistant, I joined GSI in 1965, after the medical and police verifications were over. Fortunately I sat *for the 1965 UPSC examination and was selected to the post of Jr. Geologist. I joined the office of Jr. Geologist in 1966. But one year's delay was good enough to make me junior to 140 posts held by 1964 batch Jr. Geologists (70 new recruits based on UPSC results and 70 on promotion from Assistant Geologist to Jr. Geologist as was the recruitment policy). The 70 officers from the GSI cadre were in a higher age group and they retired much earlier. But the 70 new recruits were almost of my age and the top positions were sealed by them. Even then I was promoted to the post of Director in 1991. In 2000, I was selected through departmental promotion to the post of Dy. Director General along with some others. But before we could take charge, an injunction was imposed on the DPC by the court, in relation to a court case by a group of SC/ST candidates, whose duration of service in the present post fell short of consideration zone for promotion and as a result the SC/ST cadre posts were de-reserved as per rules and some general candidates were given promotion. Though we, the senior ones in the list, were promoted against general posts, because of the court case the whole list was under injunction. The court case was continuing. As per rules, after 02 years, the DPC list got cancelled. By the time the next DPC started, I retired.*

You all heard the proverb, 'Man proposes God disposes'. Though God cannot be involved in such politics, the particular Time-Space relation plays the trick. In the previous DPC also some SC/ST posts were de-reserved, but there was no court case. But this time the Space-Time relation was different. Some SC/ST candidates, though did not complete the duration of service required for consideration, felt to make a court case - an act of a particular Time-Space. This is what is called Fate. This is not under the control of any department. It just happens. Call it accidental. Call it Fate. It is not under the control of any person/group of persons/institute. It is a play of Space-Time game. And you become a puppet. Sometime, the Space-Time game plays at per your liking, but sometime not. To survive in a nice way and to come out of any depression, the best thing is to ignore. That is possible when you hope, when you dream that good time would come. That is possible when you respect the acts of Nature.

Saibaba's 'Shraddha and Saburi' (respect and patience). Ignoring the period of sufferings and forgetting it is an elixir of life. How much space you give in your thought process is important to reach this type of elixir of life.

Space – Space - and – Space. Give long ropes to such undesired circumstances so that you enjoy their sailing away from you. And then you can enjoy your daily life under any circumstances. After all, life on Earth is for a pretty small period and the agony suffered on Earth is just short-lived compared to the eternal life of your sole which, of course, we the common people cannot perceive. But we can definitely be sure that if you are honest and active, without envying others, your sorrows or bad periods are not going to persist for long. At least, you will enjoy many soothing small fruits which will sustain your life amidst small joys and small happiness. Life will not be too disappointed. At least you can face it boldly and have good moments which will much reduce your sufferings. Mental sufferings depend on your mind and brain, not on the circumstances creating the atmosphere of sufferings. And strong and hopeful mind and brain can give you strength to endure gladly the physical sufferings. We can see from the stories of our 'Swadeshis' (those revolted against the British Rule) in jails, under inhuman tortures, that even under those wretched conditions they are joking and enjoying their daily life in the jail. This is just a mental game. And like them it becomes easier to ignore such sufferings, if you have some determinations to be achieved in your life. 'We shall overcome someday' is a strong and soothing hope.

Joint Scientific Expedition to Great Nicobar

In 1965 I joined GSI. My father would be retiring in January, 1968. What a mercy from God. At least some body is there to earn some money. I was posted in the office of West Bengal Circle on Middleton Street, Calcutta, when my boss, the Superintending Geologist (post later upgraded to Director), was Mr. C. Karunakaran. Mr. Jhingran was the Deputy Director (post later upgraded to Dy. Director General). Mr. B.C. Roy was the Director and Head of GSI (later the top post was upgraded to Director General), being placed at 27, Choringhee Road, Calcutta 700 016, the red building of Museum, rented to GSI at Re. 1 per month as the token money to retain their ownership.

Mr. Karunakaran had a tall sportsman figure, strong and stout, taking ample interests in sports and adventures. That time the Government of India was planning for a 'Joint Scientific Expedition in Great Nicobar', our southernmost island of the Andaman and Nicobar Group of Islands (more than 200 in number including a volcano on Barren Island and Refugee Settlement in the Middle Andaman – the Betapur Camp, etc.). The Andaman administration was in Port Blair on South Andaman Island. The objective of the expedition to the Virgin Island Great Nicobar ('virgin' means 'not infiltrated by the people from the main land India') was to find out whether refugee settlements would be possible in the island, presently being inhabited by two tribes Great Nicobarese and Shompen, very sparsely populated with Shompen within the interior forest areas and Nicobarese in the coastal forest areas.

It was a Joint Scientific Expedition, combining GSI, ZSI (Zoological Survey of India), BSI (Botanical Survey of India), ASI (Anthropological Survey of India) and Andaman Forest Department. Mr. Karunakaran was chosen as the Leader of the Expedition. I was selected in the GSI team in the very first year of my entry in GSI along with the senior veterans Kalyan Kumar Ray, Shyam Sundar Saha *and Parimalda (forgot the full name). The head of ZSI team was Dr. Daniel, that of BSI team was Dr. Thothatri and of ASI team was Dr. Nag.*

The expedition was scheduled from December end, 1965 to April, 1966. I was given the task of reaching Port Blair in advance in order to contact the Andaman Administration to collect 30 A-Frame small tents for officers, 05 Swiss Tents for team leaders, 14 larger A-Frame tents for laborers and storages, 01 Dome Tent for dining, 27 camp cots and 150 tarpaulins from the Betapur Settlement of Middle Andaman Island and to arrange for 40 laborers from Port Blair through the Andaman Administration. We could not get a larger supply of camp cots to accommodate the laborers also.

I skip the narration of the total episode of the expedition, involving so much hardship, tracking through dense forests, drinking water problems and solution, identification of edible herbs, protection from pythons, a miracle saving of K.K. Ray from a life-taking accident, mixed feeling to see the tombs of European members of old Galathea expedition etc.

I just narrate here in brief the four experiences in Great Nicobar Expedition.

Experience one:

We boarded the Navy ship Yerawa in Port Blair which was assigned to take us to Campbell Bay, east-central point of Great Nicobar Island. There was a small jetty for boats to anchor and walk down to the beach.

After 03 days of journey, we reached close to Campbell Bay in the noon. The ship anchored there. We had six small boats with us, tugged to the ship. We were to empty the ship before evening so that it could reach Car Nicobar, the Navy Headquarters, in the night. By the time we took out the entire luggage to the shore, it was almost evening. There were packages for 50 tents, 150 tarpaulins, 27 camp cots, dozens of boxes carrying ration for 70 persons for 05 months, office equipment and maps, equipment for geologists, zoologists, botanists, anthropologists, forest officers and personal luggage for 22 officers and 40 laborers, life jackets for all etc.

Before the sun set in, we hurriedly cleared a part of the jungle and erected a Swiss tent for Mr. Karunakaran. The ZSI, BSI and ASI teams, however, could manage to pitch 03 Swiss tents for their Leaders and a few small A-Frame tents for *the others. We four geologists of GSI and the Forest Officer from Andaman could not get time to pitch any tent for us, as we were involved in clearing the ship of all the packages brought for the expedition. Of course, the other team members invited us to share their accommodation with us. But their incomplete setting was not even sufficient for them. So, we decided to sleep on the bamboo jetty platform over the sea. We made arrangements for food for every body and after dinner we retired at around 11 PM. It was difficult to sleep on jetty platform, with the roar of the sea waves passing under the jetty and breaking down to the shore. However, we were too tired to remain awake for a long time.*

Next day we pitched tents for everybody – larger A-Frame tents to accommodate the laborers and for stores and small A-Frame tents with camp cot for each of 22 officers. We pitched the tents close to the sea shore, the inside being thickly forested. There are hundreds of holes in the sand. After I retired to the camp cot in the night, I could not ignore the sound coming out of this and that hole intermittently. I lighted the torch and found the crabs coming out of the holes. There are also coral snakes on the sea shore. That is really disturbing to think whether any coral snake would come out of the hole. For the first few nights we were much disturbed. Gradually we got habituated, consoling ourselves to leave the problem to God.

Before reaching Great Nicobar, we picked up from the Kundul Island an all-rounder man Jura to assist us in Great Nicobar. Kundul Island is just 2km north of Great Nicobar. Jura, being a Nicobarese was conversant with the coastal zones of Great Nicobar and also with movements of Great Nicobaris.

Jura came with his two kids, apparently seven years and nine years, so that thy get some good food from us. He and his sons used to sleep on a blanket spread on the sand under the open sky. One morning we saw Jura cutting logs from the jungle. Then we found that he made a high platform under the sky to use as a night bed for him and his kids. See the God's Grace. Next morning I went to Jura's platform, seeing a crowd there. I found a long and wide dead python, with the large head pierced by Jura's spear which went down deep in the ground, fixing the head tightly to the ground. And the only dog of the Campbell Bay Post of Andaman Administration (02 persons with a wireless set) remained as a corpse tightly coiled by the python. The dying python coiled the dog so strongly that all the bones were crushed. Jura told that by the cry of the dog, he woke up. Lighting the torch he saw a python coiling the dog to death (this is the practice before it would swallow the prey). Jura stroked his spear so hard that it tightly fixed the python's head to the ground. The python could not take out the head from the ground. The dying python pressed the dog in its coil so hard that the dog became 'kima' (smashed meat).

We got a shock. Had Jura not made the platform for the night stay, the same fate could be met by his sons, or, by himself.

God is everywhere to save us, if we need to be saved. Just a day before this incidence, it came to Jura's mind to erect the platform. Is it a coincidence? Or, a secret directive by God, influencing his mind to act accordingly. When you are blessed, Nature conspires to save you.

Experience Two:

Initially we carried out the geological traverses from Campbell Bay, before shifting the camp to other places. One day it was decided that to cover the geological studies of a particular segment, myself, Shyamda (to call an elder brother we suffix 'da' after the name) and Parimalda would take the traverse through the forest northward, then curving to the east to a decided point on the sea shore. And Kalyanda would take a boat to examine the rocks along the coast and would reach the determined point within 3 PM so that we track back through the forest before the evening. And the boatman would take the boat back to Campbell Bay. Early morning we three along with four laborers tracked through the jungle in the set direction taking help of compass, keeping signs on the trees at intervals for guiding our return journey. We examined the rocks in the visibility and reached the decided point on the sea shore in time. There was no sign of Kalyanda, or, his boatman. We waited for an hour. Then we rushed back to the camp to form a search party with men from GSI and ZSI (they had rifles). We forwarded following the same path and shouting taking their names. After crossing half the distance we heard footsteps on dried leaves from the east. Then we found Kalyanda and driver Kurup, limping forward in a distressed condition. Their whole body is with blood stains. We helped them in coming back to the camp. After some rest, Kalyanda narrated that after going half the distance of our meeting point, Kalyanda saw a big rock cliff. He directed Kurup, who was rowing the boat, to approach the rock cliff. When they were close to the rock cliff, suddenly a big wave came and threw the boat hard on the rock cliff. The boat smashed into pieces. Luckily, they were thrown over the rock cliff on to the sand, rolling over several times. They were with lot of bruises, by rubbing with sand and blood was coming through the bruises. What a planning! Kurup, our jeep driver in Port Blair, was taken as a boat driver, without having the experience of driving a boat along the shore.

It was again God's grace that they were saved. Had they not been thrown over the cliff, their heads would be broken into pieces like the boat.

Amidst the hardship there were pleasures also. We were camping in Pulobaha. There were coral reef platforms at places. While taking the geological traverses along these parts of the coast during the time of high tides, Jura used to become a fish catcher for us. During high tides with sea waves moving over the coral reefs, lot of fishes used to come along with the sea water. At the time the water was receding back, we could see the fishes clearly, moving along with the receding water. Jura used to catch them by throwing his spear, tied with a rope to his left hand. The throw used to be very accurate, holding the fish. His targets were larger fishes; say half a kilo size, so that aiming became better. He used to make a garland of the fishes around his neck with the help of a jungle creeper which he used as a string. There were lots of creepers in the jungle.

During lunch time Jura used to climb up the coconut trees which were plenty along the coast and bring down the green coconuts, full of water and pulp/kernel. Some time, when the drinking water finished, we used to cut pieces of thick canes and immediately holding them upright on the open mouth to consume the water flowing out of the cane pieces. At least one glass of water would be available from each piece.

Experience Three

That time we were camping in Casurina Bay, on the western coast of Great Nicobar, just opposite to Campbell Bay. We did not cut across the forest to the western coast. That was not possible in this dense forest, forbidding even the flow of the sunrays at places. There would be ample chance to lose the right track, as you cannot go straight following the compass direction because of the presence of jungles of thorny bushes at places, where you are to side-track them and then correcting your path to reach the destination. And camping inside the dense forest without proper arrangements would be suicidal. There were no ferocious animals like tigers and lions. But there were lot of pythons and poisonous snakes, large lizards, crocodiles not only in the sea, but also in the inner marshy lands etc.

And that would not serve our purpose. We were to cover the geological studies, moving across the coast and then taking cross traverses inside. Our small steamer Choulanga used to take us from one point on the coast to another chosen point at an interval of 10 to 15 days as pre-planned, because the ship would leave our team of four geologists and four laborers at the decided point and go away to shift other camps to their destinations. Thus, for ten/fifteen days we would remain cut-off from civilization, without having any communication outside. That time we did not have any satellite phone. No question was there for any outside help in case of any accident, or, health hazard. If somebody would die, there was no choice but to put the body in a grave, with a caption wrapped by a plastic cover and tied on a tree, or, a chiseled gravestone, if available: 'Here lies the body of ……', like the tomb of two of the participants in the old Galathea Expedition in Great Nicobar.

We were very pleased in staying in Casurina Bay. Firstly, myself and Karunakaran from GSI and the full teams of ZSI, BSI, ASI and Andaman Forest were together again. Secondly, Jura used to go to the sea shore in the night with a torch and a hand-made sword. And he used to come back after an hour or so with a large bunch of Lobsters (big sea prawns). 'Was it a magic! Jura how was it possible?' Jura explained in his broken Hindi that the prawns come to the shore in the night to scale-off (leaving the body scales like snakes and cockroaches at intervals). They do not move seeing the torch light. Rest is easy. After all, it was a virgin island. The lobsters did not have experience of being killed by the people.

However, our joyful days were short-lived. Our only ship Choulanga was not with us. It was sent to Car Nicobar for some repairs – one day's journey from Campbell Bay. But it did not turn up by the scheduled date. With so many people, the ration was depleting very fast. There *was no way to bring ration from our store in Campbell Bay. When the ration stood just for two more days of service, Mr. Karunakaran asked me to take some laborers and track to the north following the coast, then lit a fire to attract the people from the Kundul Island, just 2 km north of Great Nicobar. If they come with a boat being attracted by the fire, then we were to go with them to Kundul, purchase rice (available in Kundul) and come back to Casurina Bay by tracking back. Kalyanda, Shyamda and Parimalda were staying in Kundul Island in order to cover the geological studies of the northern part of Great Nicobar by coming from Kundul.*

The distance from Casurina Bay to the northern end of Great Nicobar is around 25 km. So, we were to make night halt somewhere close to the coast. However, I was not allowed to go alone. Dr. Daniel and one more person from ZSI, Dr. Thothatri from BSI joined me. We started next morning, taking four laborers, carrying 100 chapati (Indian homemade bread) for our food along with a few tin stuffs and a mixture of rice and dal (lentil) with the idea that if we would fail to attract Kundul people, or, our team at Kundul, we were to track back to Casurina Bay and we would take Khhichri (rice and lentil cooked in water along with some spices) on the way back.

It was not a difficult journey along the coast. Once the problem came, when the coast was blocked by a jungle of thorny bushes. We diverted the journey and came back again to the coast after crossing the jungle of thorny bushes. At one point we were to go through sea water, knee deep, where sea formed an estuary. By seeing us a crocodile jumped to the sea from the opposite bank of the estuary and swimming at a distance of around 30 m from us. Mentally we were comfortable, as the Zoologist had a loaded gun.

In the afternoon we reached a place where we found bamboo platforms not far from the coast. Such platforms were made by the Nicobarese people for temporary shelter while moving from one place to the other. A number of big round glass jars were kept at the base of coconut trees with a wooden funnel around the tree trunk, the end resting on the jar. When it rained, water got collected in the jars. That was their cooking and drinking water. Glass jars were found on the shore. I personally collected four. After consumption of wines, the ships usually throw the empty glass jars to the sea.

Some of them, while floating, are driven to the shore of different islands.

The first thing we did after settling was to go to the sea for a bath. Mr. Thothatri sat at around 5m away from the shoreline, putting some oil on the body and rubbing it. We were sitting further up and gossiping. The idea was to land to the sea after Thothatri finished his oil message. Suddenly a large wave came, pushed up Thothatri close to us. The next moment he was slipping down the sand along with water. We captured his hands. He was lying flat with the back on the sand. Then we realized the mistake we made in trying to take bath in such a high gradient sea shore. Had Thothatri not taken the oil message and we then straightway went into the sea, we would be taken to the deep water by such high sea waves. However, we tried to wash our body in the waves rolled over to us. It was more of sand and less of water, as we did not dare to go further down. After the day's hard journey through sand, we relished the sand bath. Not bad. In the villages of Rajasthan, I have seen the cooking utensils and the steel plates shining after getting washed by sand; no water to get the luxury of washing plates in those desert regions. Of course, I do not know whether the germs can be cleared off the plate through cleaning by sand.

Next morning we started and reached the northern end of Great Nicobar at about 11 AM. We were fortunate to see Kalyanda and Shyamda who already reached there for geological studies. The boat could not accommodate all of us in. We made two trips. We were 8 persons and then Kalyanda, Shyamda and their boatman, totaling to 11 persons. I still remember, with 5 or 6 persons at a time the boat dipped into the water further and there was a hole on one side which was then below the sea level. As a result water started pouring in. And with equal speed, we were throwing the water out with the help of two mugs.

From Kundul we could send a wireless message to the ship. It came next evening. We purchased rice, flour and other necessary items from Kundul and went straight to Casurina Bay, where the half starving people were waiting for us.

Experience Four

Our expedition got closed in the last week of April, 1966. The Navy ship Yerawa was scheduled to reach Campbell

Bay on 03.05.1966 morning. We closed the accounts on 02.05.1966 and the ration was closed, keeping a small provision for the breakfast on the 3rd of May. Before the dawn we started gathering the boxes, tarpaulins etc. at one place close to the jetty. But there is no trace of the ship. We were unable to send any message to the ship. The whole day passed. The whole night passed. We had to reopen the food containers. But this time the food preparation was centralized at one place. On 4th May at around 3 PM the radio message came to the Campbell Bay Post that due to bad weather the ship could not locate Great Nicobar and diverted towards Sumatra. For shortage of drinking water, the ship was now heading for Car Nicobar.

It was not clear when the ship would be able to reach Campbell Bay. It was a critical situation, because with further delay it would be difficult for our small ship Choulanga to cross the 10° channel under rough May weather in this part of Indian Ocean. Neither we could leave our small ship to be completely stranded. We tried, through Campbell Bay Post Wireless System, to contact Car Nicobar and Nan cowry offices of Akuji Group to charter a ship. But the contact could not be made. Neither we were having sufficient ration for this great family of around 65 persons (including Jura and his two sons) to sustain for another month.

We discussed the pros and cons. It was decided that Mr. Karunakaran, Dr. Daniel, Dr. Thothatri, myself along with Kalyanda, Shyamda and 26 laborers would board Choulanga and reach Car Nicobar to charter a ship for 16 officers and 14 laborers staying then in Campbell Bay. This would reduce the pressure on ration and there would be a way to come out of Great Nicobar.

The problem now was with Jura and his two kids – how to send them back to Kundul. He was not inclined to stay further in Great Nicobar. Choulanga had the problem with the compressor of the ship. The captain was telling that he would not be able to stop at Kundul. The present condition of Choulanga would allow it to start the engine maximum three times. It could not be rectified in Car Nicobar. So, leaving us in Car Nicobar, the ship would straightway head for Port Blair. It was decided that Jura with his two kids would be in his boat, the boat being tied up with the rear end railing of the ship. Reaching close to Kundul, the rope would be unfastened and Jura would row his boat to Kundul. It would be a journey within 30 km, taking around 4.5 hours for Choulanga to pass Kundul.

Early morning with personal luggage we boarded Choulanga. There were 02 cabins, with one berth in a cabin and 02 berths in the second cabin. These were occupied by Mr. Karunakaran, Dr. Daniel and Dr. Thothatri. On the deck were 06 benches. These were occupied in advance by the laborers. In this rough sea they did not bother to wait for us to occupy any bench. We three then brought 09 tin boxes, with 03 boxes placed in a row between the benches which became our bed. In fact it was a better arrangement than sitting on the benches in this rolling sea.

The journey started. We saw poor Jura sitting straight and holding tightly the hull of the boat, which was moving fast with the ship, at times with short jumps. Only the experts can manage hull in such rough journeys. His alertness would save the boat from turning upside down. However, we were keeping a close watch on them. The two kids were lying on the boat to have a better grip. They were holding the sides of the boat tightly. The worst part was that after three hours of journey the rain started. We understood, Jura was so much alert to save the kids that he did not bother anything else except having full grip on the hull. After 5 hours of journey we saw the island Kundul. The ship was running slow, taking concern of Jura. When we were close to the island, the rope, tying the boat, was released. Suddenly the boat slowed down. We waved to Jura and he reciprocated with a smile. We saw Jura rowing towards the island, after taking the rope from the sea. It was a very sad moment for us to miss the company of such a devoted brave person. Perhaps we would not meet again.

Thank God. Jura could escape in time. It was raining only. After two hours, storm started along with rains. We were unable to sit, as the rolling of the ship was making us sick. Mr. Karunakaran advised us not to be in empty stomach. That would give us more nausea. But who would cook food? Nobody was in a condition to cook food, not even the veteran crew members of the ship. Fortunately we had cans of biscuits. Everybody, including the crew, ate biscuits. The crew, specially the Master, was very busy in controlling the ship.

With the storm the real problem started. When the waves were coming from the front, for a moment we were practically within the sea. With the water flushing out, again we could see the sky. But that moment was shocking, too shocking. We were afraid, too afraid whether the ship was going down the sea. The side waves were tolerable. The waves were falling on the deck and flashing out through the holes. Water was flowing around our beds and with the next tilt of the ship it was going out through the holes. The beds, with us on them, were moving to and fro on the boxes with the continuous rolling of the ship. But Master of the ship was avoiding the side waves by steering the ship continuously, because with more powerful side waves the ship might be toppled. That situation, of course, did not come. But whatever we faced, it was good enough to shatter our mental strength. We did not have any such experience in our life.

Kalyanda came so many times to the Andaman Group of islands, but this time he fell sick, vomiting a number of times. By 3 PM we reached Car Nicobar. Here the sea was not that turbulent. The Akuji's ship, which was in Car Nicobar and which we planned to charter, left Car Nicobar just half an hour before. We were in no mood to follow it without taking some rest and without taking food. The local administration arranged for cooking food for us.

With one hour in Car Nicobar, we boarded Choulanga, heading for Nan Cowry. After treatment by a doctor, Kalyanda was feeling better. The main medicine was the food for us. We reached Nan Cowry in the evening, but could not catch Akuji's ship. We decided to stay in Nan Cowry and try to charter a ship for Campbell Bay. Next morning we bed good bye to Choulanga. It headed for Port Blair.

After a day's trial we could charter a ship. Next morning it headed for Campbell Bay. And we occupied a cargo ship and managed to make beds in the spaces available between rows of cargos. Next day we reached Port Blair. After three days the rest of the Party arrived.

Now it is a golden memory of sea adventure and adventure in a virgin island. But that time it was shocking at times. If Choulanga was defeated by the stormy sea of 10° channels, the ship along with us would rest on the sea floor. What would happen to my old parents having no money to fight the situation out! God is great. He saved us from the calamities.

Short Stay in Odisha

My fourth sister's marriage took place in February, 1966. That time I was in Great Nicobar. I could not attend the function. But I could make some financial contribution. That was the only console. I am closer to my fourth sister. Out of my four sisters only the third and the fourth sisters are alive now at the age of 81 and 79. I would be 74 on 2nd January, 2015.

My father had a cerebral attack in December, 1966. Hard work and anxieties for the family's upkeep played its role now. I was in Bankura, engaged in search for base metals in a favorable geological environment. I got the news on the second day and rushed back to Calcutta. Within six months father recovered from the partial paralyses of the left side. But the vigor never was like past. The main problem was that his mental strength got reduced after the cerebral attack. He would be retiring in January, 1968. That made his mind restless.

However, after his physical recovery, peace came again in our house. But I was transferred to Odisha Circle of GSI in Bhubaneswar in September, 1967. My first assignment was in systematic geological mapping in parts of Kalahandi district along with my senior colleague Mr. R.N. Sinha Roy (Ramenda). He was an open hearted jolly fellow.

On 24th November (taken from my diary) I and Ramenda started from Bhubaneswar by train and reached Kesinga. Up to 29th November we were in Kesinga. Kesinga was especially in my remembrance, as the 26th of November was a special day for me, when my parents and uncles performed the blessing ceremony for my bride before the wedding which was fixed on the 6th of March, 1968.

Our first camp was planned at Koksara, around 105km from Kesinga via Bhawanipatna, the headquarters of Kalahandi district. But the train connection was up to Kesinga. That time we had no vehicle with us from GSI, because of the strike of the drivers. And there was strict restriction to drive any

Government vehicle by us. We went by bus to Bhawanipatna from Kesinga, the fare being Rs. 1.25 per person (a distance of 35km). From Kesinga we hired a truck to Koksara.

This time there was a crisis in production of rice in India and there was temporary ban on transport of rice from one state to the other without permit. As a result there was black-marketing of rice in Calcutta, with Rs. 3.00 per kg, but in Koksara it was Re 1.00 for 1.5kg of the same quality of rice. Ten eggs cost Re 1.00 in Koksara; milk Re 1.00 for 2ltrs. Ghee (melted butter) was Rs. 10.00 per kg. Life was composed; no hurry to do anything.

We were in Inspection Bungalow. There was a Block Development Office, a small health center with an ambulance (not thought of in those days in such remote places) and a post office. It was decided that every alternate day I would post a letter to my father who also would repeat the same process. Then we did not have any mobile or STD facilities in India. Where the telephone exchanges were available (in the district headquarters only), we could try for phone calls, at times by sitting for hours to get a connection.

We had a problem in collecting rock samples, while mapping the area around Koksara. There was not even a single outcrop without human soil on it, some were dry, some were still wet. This was and still a big issue in India even now in 2014. It is not because the villagers could not and cannot afford to erect a small toilet. It is mainly due to the age old practice in India that they go to the field in clearing the rectum. The Africans even in backward places like DRC (Democratic Republic of Congo) and the Republic of Congo are very poor in general, but they are having at least a make shift toilet, by digging a well and erecting a wooden or a bamboo platform on it with a hole. In India, while camping at the fringe of any village, we saw ladies going together to the open ground outside the villages, sitting close to each other, gossiping, while doing that great performance.

On December 7, we shifted to Ladoo Gaon by bullock cart, a distance of 7km from Koksara. Even in such interiors, there was the business community Marwaris. By seeing their modesty, tolerance, patience and accommodative efforts to the living conditions of each place, one would understand why they flourished in business. Even now the accessibility was so poor. And they were here for the last four generations (including the generation of children). Their main income here was farming and transport. Of course, everything was not in an honest way. They used to give advance to the poor farmers and in return they used to purchase rice from them at a rate much lower than the market price. Illiteracy became a curse for the farmers. That time there was not much vigilance from the Forest Department of the Government of India, or, from the State Forest Department regarding illegal trading of Forest Products. These people took advantage of staying in the interiors of Kalahandi district and got engaged in collecting Forest Products and timbers and bamboos from the Forest area without any permit.

There was no toilet. We erected N-tents for arranging make- shift toilets, by cutting trenches and filling up each day's excretions by soil. Bathing was under open sky on a platform. There was an outside half-broken shade for kitchen.

We were taking long traverses, around 15 miles (24km) a day to cover up the mapping fast. The market day was once in a week. We used to purchase vegetables for the week.

For a few days, we shifted to Pujarigura, staying in a Panchayat Bhawan. This was a big hall. First day, after coming from the field, when we took out our apparels, given for drying under the sun, we found a number of caterpillars on the underside. Same thing happened on the next day. Otherwise we did not notice any caterpillar in the area. They must be coming from some trees.

Next night, I just slept. A shout from Ramenda woke me up. He pointed to a caterpillar on the floor. What happened? Ramenda woke up by feeling the touch of fingers in the hair. For a moment he thought that his wife was putting her fingers through his hair. Then he realized that it was the field where he was now. He brushed his fingers swiftly through the hair. The caterpillar fell on the floor. While we were talking, I saw another caterpillar crawling on the bed. It was removed. That night we had disturbed sleep. Next morning we searched the place to find out wherefrom the caterpillars were coming. Oh my God! Practically the whole ceiling of wood and bamboos were covered by caterpillars and their cocoons. So, they are the caterpillars to be transformed to butterflies. We may hold the butterflies affectionately, but certainly not the caterpillars. So, we immediately packed up the belongings and left for Ladoo Gaon, to cover the mapping of this part from there.

The next place of work was around Ampanighat ('Ampani' means small tiger, i.e., leopard) and around Karlapat ('Karla' means big tiger). That time a man-eater (tiger) was reported from the Kalahandi district. We hired a local shikari (hunter). We met the collector and he agreed to send us report, if any, of the movement of the man-eater, through the bus driver.

I remember, once crossing two hill chains we were on the top of the third chain. We were tired and thirsty. Seeing a spring, we rushed to the place. The shikari stopped us and pointed to some pockmarks (footprints), where slowly the side water was pouring. He whispered, 'just now a tiger has left the place, may be due to our noise. Better we leave quickly.'

Even in such remote places on the plateau, we saw local people, may be 4 to 8 huts, living heartily. But, at places they also built up small accommodations on the trees. Nice place – wide flat land, surrounded by jungles, enough spring water, wild flowers.

In the last week of December, 1967, I bed good bye to Ramenda, while going on long leave. On 6th March, 1968 I got married. The date of birth of my wife Dipti was unique – the 15th August of 1947, the day of independence of India. She is a sweet lady, jolly, versatile and composed. As per Indian style, her name changed from Dipti Aich to Dipti Sarkar. But we called her Dipa, as the name of our eldest sister was Dipti.

I narrated all these events of Great Nicobar and Odisha to narrate that if the mind is composed, one can enjoy the stay in every situation. You can enjoy the changing beauties of the different places, if you try to love the places and the people living there.

Rajasthan

Within a month of our wedding, I was selected to join, on deputation, the Airborne Mineral Surveys and Exploration Wing (AMSE) under the Ministry of Steel and Mines with posting in Jaipur, Rajasthan. It was a new department formed under the Ministry of Mines. The Jaipur office of AMSE was temporarily located in Himanshu Bhawan of GSI in Bani Park.

Through my friends in GSI, Jaipur, I was able to fix a house on rent in C-Scheme, Jaipur. So, we - I, my wife, father and mother and my younger brother Mihir, left the Calcutta accommodation and boarded the train Toofan Express to have the break journey in Agra. The luggage, weighing 857 kg in 52 packets, was booked in the accompanying parcel van. Next morning we got down at Agra, in order to take the train to Jaipur next day. The

TT came and wanted to examine the luggage receipt. Then he wanted to weigh the luggage. We had to pay the porters to take the luggage to the parcel office. They weighed and told us that 10kg was extra. Then he told us that as per rule, we had to pay for 867kg afresh along with fines from Calcutta to Jaipur. I hesitated, doubting their observations and told them that the luggage was weighed in Howrah station by the railway staff and as per their bill, I had paid. "Nothing doing. You are to pay now, if you want the luggage for shifting to the hotel. Otherwise give me Rs. 100.00. I would permit you to take the luggage." Thank God. In the meantime, a constable came there. Seeing him, he told me to go to the hotel and he would collect money that evening. We went to the hotel joyfully that we were now out of his grip. Next morning, I was taking a shave in the bathroom, when my wife knocked at the door. 'Darling. He has come". 'Who?' 'That TT from the Railway Station'. I realized that at least one of the three Tungawalas who carried the luggage must have told him which hotel we checked in. I came out and told, 'It is good that you have come. I have been told by my boss that whatever amount I am to pay to the railways for the luggage and fines, let me pay. Please take the amount and give me a receipt'. For a moment he remained silent and then told me, 'O.K. Mr. Sarkar. Please pay then in Jaipur. The date is over. I cannot take the money now'. Many times I moved between Howrah and Jaipur via Agra and he had never failed to recognize my face.

After reaching Jaipur we saw a white big van Traveller waiting for us in the station. It was thrilling, thinking of the jeeps given by GSI for travel of Geologists. Jaipur station building was very artistic, looking like a pink fort. All the buildings in the old city of Jaipur were pink in color. Jaipur was called the Pink City. Similarly, Udaipur was called the White City, all the buildings being white.

Next day I went to AMSE office in Himanshu Bhawan. I found only the key of the office door waiting for me. There was absolutely no body in the AMSE office. I then met the Superintending Geologist, GSI to ask whom I was to give my charge report. He advised me to call to AMSE, Delhi for advice. They advised me to sign the charge report and keep it with me. I was told to wait for a month in Jaipur. Then I alone went to Delhi. Mr. S.K. Srivastava, Sr. Geologist already accommodated 02 Geologists (B. Sharma and M. Singh) in his 2BHK house. He accommodated me also. We used to sleep in the Drawing room which was quite large. Mr. Srivastava, his wife, two grown up kids and his mother were all in the house and then three of us. But Mrs. Srivastava welcomed us joyfully. It was a nice accommodative family. A bright example of large space in the heart (I remember, once in Dusehra festival, we were 21 people in that house). After a month, we were able to find out individual accommodations for us in Greater Kailash. We brought our families to Delhi.

We were to work under Operation Hardrock to take part in multi-sensor airborne geophysical surveys over Aravalli and Delhi Fold belts and the ground follow up in search of base metals (copper, lead and zinc and associated metals).

We conducted the airborne geophysical surveys from Jaipur, Alwar and Udaipur. Every evening was the period of flight path recovery on photo mosaic and anomaly plotting, and then marking the anomalous belts. One evening we were waiting for the Geophysicist to bring the film to us. That day he came with a heavy face, 'Boys. After the flying was over, we found that we forgot to load the film in the camera. So we lost today's contractual money from AMSE'.

Then the ground follow up started. First we camped in Khetri, close to Khetri Copper Mine, checking the airborne anomalies on ground and trying to find out the causative body for the anomaly. We detected sulphides (mainly copper) in Banwas between Kolihan and Madan Khudan Mines and another pocket north of Madan Khudan. A party started doing detailing.

A search party, including me, moved to the Bhilwara district in 1970. It was one of the best periods in our life. It was a big camp of geologists and geophysicists. We enjoyed the food prepared by housewives of different food habits – from Bengal, Uttar Pradesh, Punjab, Haryana, Tamil Nadu and Kerala. We used to go for survey early in the morning and returning by afternoon. We had pack lunch with us. But we enjoyed the dinner together under the canopy of two tents, pitched end to end. After the food, at least one hour we used to be together, reciting, singing, storytelling, jokes and indoor games including housie, three cards & bridge, rummy, chess, ludo, carom etc.

There we detected a new Lead – Zinc belt in Dedwas area, parallel to Rajpura Dariba Lead – Zinc belt and a small Copper belt in Banera Reserve Forest on north-east of Dedwas belt. Both the belts are in the same alignment, together named as Pur – Banera belt. There was also a magnetite deposit west of Dedwas lead – zinc belt. I was given the charge of test drilling in these belts. Another small copper deposit was found in the south-western part of this belt.

I stayed in Bhilwara up to the middle of 1974. I was back to Calcutta to stay there up to the middle of 1991. Then, on promotion to the post of Director, GSI I was posted to Raipur in Chhattisgarh region of the then Madhya Pradesh state.

I was actually selected for posting in Coal Wing, GSI, Calcutta. But, a group of seniors was able to keep the post in Coal Wing for someone favored by them, thereby shunting me out to Raipur.

Here also I felt the hands of God (and of my Guru – you cannot separate the wish of God from the wish of True Saints) on my head. The stay in Raipur was a boon to my career as a Geologist. This I would narrate later on.

I retired from GSI in February, 2002. But my career as a geologist did not stop there. I believe, all these happened because of a planning by God, which was initiated with my undesired posting to Raipur. This has been narrated under chapter on 'Fortunate to Receive Special Blessing from Thakur Baba'.

Before I narrate this part of my career, I am to tell in brief of the hands of God on me through my Gurus.

Helping Hands

In my life I was fortunate to closely meet two enlightened saints – 'Siddha Purush/Rishi'). In religious bodies, what I have seen, 'Sanyasi' (a holy man taking shelter under religious activities leaving the domestic life) is gradually promoted to higher positions, becoming 'Mandaleswar' (Chief of the religious body). They may be religious, honest, active, loving persons, but that does not mean that they are enlightened, attaining the highest position of the spiritual life, having no material desire and having the realization of God. The enlightened saints become spiritually powerful, though normally they do not like to show any of their spiritual powers, but at certain time of need, to overcome some drastically bad situation of their devotees, their powers get flashed. That time the devotees can feel the touch of powers of these Great

Souls. They are Enlightened Saints, like 'Thakur Ramkrishna' – not Mandaleswar or Shankaracharyas by designation. Adi Shankaracharya, of course, was a Great Enlightened Saint. Their only job is to think and act for the welfare of the devotees and of the world and the rest of the time just to be absorbed in God's presence through highest stage of meditation ('samadhi). And their love for the people! I have not experienced such all-out immense love from anybody else – not even from the parents.

True Saints are there to guide you without any self-interest and rescue you in your need. The Forces of Nature conspire to carry out their blessings, provided you surrender to them, have faith in them and have patience – Sirdee Saibaba's 'Shraddha and Saburi' (Respect and Patience). Of course, we have heard from the holy people and also read that there are Great Enlightened Saints in the Higher Himalayas, beyond Gomukh, beyond the level of accessibility of common people. Rarest of rare of them are in 'samadhi' (completely absorbed in meditation without any outward senses) for years and they do not take any food or water. Their body takes the life energy from air itself.

For God's sake, do not mix up the truly enlightened saints with saffron cloth cladded religion-oriented service/business class who make tricks to falsely decipher that they are enlightened and near to God. These people are full of desire like us; the only difference is that we are leading a family life with a wife, but they are not having a legal wife. In Jashpur where I am staying now, lot of such persons wearing saffron cloth come to us for alms, mainly cash and in the afternoon they spend part of the money to purchase ganja and daru (wine) and, if available, a company of opposite sex. They say that they are 'Brahmachari' (bachelor and not indulged in sex). Most of them come from Nasik and Ujjain. One of them rang me from there for a financial help. I overheard his conversation with his wife and children. I believe, though they earn, presenting false pictures, they are not that harmful for the society like the big traders with malpractices, even involving duplicate medicines, urea water in the name of milk, adulteration in foods, doctors exploiting patients. So, when they come for alms, I admit them.

You will find that in India, many small new temples come up, being located in nice places along any river, lake, on hills close to some small towns. You ask them regarding their administration. Always, you will get the answer that they belong to certain religious sects/communities. These sects spread their centers of operation by building new centers and deploying a so called saint there. During my presence in Jashpur district, one such saint was arrested by police for charge of rape (a minor girl). He was convicted and jailed. These so called religious clans/sects are nothing but traders in the name of religion.

There is no harm in spreading the religious centers, provided it is done following some ethics. The common people have the generosity to visit the temples and offer whatever they can afford. No body minds for spending in the interest of the temple development and in the interest of the priests. Many centers offer food either free or at a low cost to the devotees visiting the temples. But there are many small centers in and around villages and small towns, where by taking advantage of innocence and ignorance of the simple villagers, the dishonest priests cheat them in the name of religion and god and in presenting a bad picture of their future.

I have narrated these pictures not to insult them, but to present the difference, when I mention of some enlightened saints, in the true sense of the term. Many foreigners come to India, meet such persons in disguise of saints, as mentioned above and comment that the saints in India are a group of hoax.

Having narrated that, I come to the point of our discussion regarding Touch of Helping Hands in Life. Most of the time you will feel the touch of the helping hands of God through some persons, or, through some environments /phenomena which happen to be created in your favor and you get relieved. If you analyze, you will find that the main purpose of such help is to give some relief to you from the financial burden, from the mental burden, to bring back happiness in your life, to caution you against your present planning which may put you in troubles etc.

Well, the introduction has become larger than life. I narrate here some of the events which cannot be explained by any reasoning based on science.

Shri Shri Swami Dhyananda Maharaj

श्री श्री मৎ स्वামী ध्यানানन्द महाराज

Shri Shri Mat Swami Dhyananda Maharaj

শিষ্য-শিষ্যা পরিবেষ্টিত স্বামী ধ্যানানন্দ মহারাজ
ছবিটি কোন্নগর আশ্রমে প্রায় ৪৫ বছর আগে তোলা ॥

The photo was taken in 1960 at
Konnagar Ashram (Hermitage).
Sadhubaba with the disciples.

শ্রী শ্রী মৎ স্বামী ধ্যানানন্দ মহারাজ

Our family was fortunate to be always under the shelter of a Guru (enlightened saint). During my childhood days in present Bangla Desh, there was an Ashram, called Belphulia Ashram by the river Bhairav in Khulna district. Shri Shri Swami Dhyanananda Maharaj was the Enlightened Saint living there. My maternal grandfather and grandmother were his close disciples. Swami Dhyanananda was the Great Disciple of Shrimat Pranabananda Swami, the Founder of the renowned social body Bharat Sevashram. Some of the close disciples have witnessed the touch of his helping hands and narrated in a book on him.

In domestic life, the name of Swami Dhyanananda was Kamadaprasanna Choudhury, a member of the Aristocrat Zaminder family of Village Bhawanipur at the junction of the rivers Atreyi and Yamuna in East Bengal (present Bangladesh). During the month of June-July, Atreyi was flowing with high current. A boat carrying his beloved daughter Prabhabati and his elder brother Kashinath Choudhury along with some other persons was coming to Bhawanipur from the house of Prabhabati's husband, only a few days after marriage. The year was perhaps 1926. The purpose was to meet her grandmother (mother of Kamadaprasanna and Kashinath), who wished to see her before going to the holy place Banaras to spend the rest of her life there. Just a mile before reaching Bhawanipur, a storm broke. The boat sank. Prabhabati embraced her uncle. Kashinath tried to swim to the shore, holding tightly Prabhabati. But due to the strong current, his grip got loosened and Prabhabati flowed away. Everybody came to the shore, except Prabhabati. Her body was recovered and brought back to their house in Bhawanipur. Kamadaprasanna got the greatest shock of his life by seeing the dead body of his beloved daughter.

The ever vibrating Kamadaprasanna became as silent as a rock. The only question engulfing him was where the Soul goes after death. He could not continue his stay in the family. In 1927 he gifted his properties to his family and other dependents and made proper arrangements for his family to get interest on bank deposits and the monthly rents from accommodations given on rent. By taking permission from wife, son and friends he left the house. He went to Banaras and took the permission of his mother. Then he went to Gaya. He stayed there and started meditation in Tapoban (forest area marked for meditation) near

the place Kapildhara. Only once in a day
he used to take food by cooking himself
and the rest of the time he was engaged
in meditation. After a year, he started
his pilgrimage and reached close to the
village Ladi (pronunciation Larri), around
125miles from Kapildhara. On the hilly
truck he saw a Shiva Mandir. The priest
of the temple handed over the charge of
the temple to him and left the place. For
one year he worshiped the Shiva along
with his meditation. Now he started
longing for 'Nirakar Sadhana' (deep
meditation on the true nature of God as
Super consciousness without any shape).
He left the place in search of Ultimate
Truth. During his pilgrimage he met a
Saint near a Hill named Barabar. He
wanted to baptize (to give 'diksha') him.
But Kamadaprasanna denied, saying
that without the instruction from God
Shiva, he would not accept 'Diksha'. The
saint said, under the order from Shiva,
he was there to give him 'Diksha'. By
hearing this Kamadaprasanna startled.
The mantra was 'sohang' (I am He – He
means God). Kamadaprasanna said that
he was not fit for that. The Saint said,
if you are not fit, then who else would
be fit for that. Kamadaprasanna started
uttering the Bijmantra, completely in
'samadhi'. Twenty four days passed in
the same position. Next day he gradually

came out of 'samadhi'. The body was very weak. He was unable to move for a distance. In the meantime, a farmer came with some food. He took it.

He went back to Gaya, staying in Bharat Sevashram. Shrimat Pranabananda Swami then advised him to go to Khulna in East Bengal to take charge of Belphulia Ashram. Here he started deeper meditations. He left all clothes except the loin cloth. He became silent ('mounabrata'), without uttering any word. During this time Shrimat Pranabananda Swami gave him 'sanyas' (introducing in the life of a saint) in Bajitpur Sevashram, naming him 'Swami Dhyananda'.

For twelve years he remained silent and was under meditation. At last the day came when he became enlightened. In 1942 onward he started giving 'diksha' to his disciples.

After Independence, Khulna and Jessore districts went to Pakistan. Most of the disciples of Baba came to India. At the request of disciples, he agreed for an Ashram in India. An Ashram was established in Konnagar, close to Calcutta. It is located on Bankim Chatterjee Street, at the back side of the Housing Complex.

The Ashram was inaugurated by Baba in 1954. Up to 1969 he used to look after both the Ashrams of Belphulia and Konnagar, as many of his disciples were still in East Bengal (East Pakistan). In August, 1960 he came permanently to Konnagar Ashram. On the 28th Magh, 1367 of the Bengali calendar (1961 of the English calendar), before dawn, breaking his routine, he came out of his underground meditation room and wakened up every body. He advised them to finish the daily morning worship. He himself distributed 'prasad'. He looked after their lunch. After evening worship and prayers, he himself made arrangements for the dinner. He distributed the meals to the disciples. After the dinner he bed good bye to them and closed the door of his room (not locked). On morning of next day the disciples found his body lying still on bed. He left the body.

The Belphulia Ashram was a center for social activities in addition to religious/ spiritual activities. There was a school also under the ashram. These activities were not possible in the small space of Konnagar Ashram. But this never disturbed his mental peace. He was above all desires. In the night he used to be in meditation. In the day he used to be with the disciples.

It was the 20ᵗʰ May of 1957, at around 10 AM. He was sitting in Konnagar Ashram. Suddenly his body leaned against the wall, unconscious. The disciples got shocked. But Guruma, who used to look after Baba as a great disciple right from the initial days in Belphulia Ashram, was aware of such situations. She comforted others saying, "Baba has temporarily left the body and has gone somewhere else". The reason was known after a few days. That day, at that time a disciple in Calcutta met a fatal accident and was admitted unconscious in the Medical College and Hospital, Calcutta. After regaining consciousness, he was searching around and asking, 'Where is Baba? Why am I in hospital? What happened to me? So long I was lying on the lap of my Gurudev'. His left hand broke badly. The doctors were afraid that it might be amputated. He was brought to Konnagar Ashram. Baba gave a divine smile and touched his left hand. After the next x-ray the doctors found that the bone pieces were found joined as if it was never broken. The doctors claimed, 'It is miracle!'

As I told, my maternal grandfather and grandmother were his great disciple right from 1940 or before that. I was born in 1941. I was a mere child that time, not knowing much of 'Baba's Bibhuti. One incident I remember. It was perhaps in 1947 beginning. I was recovered from Typhoid after ayurvedic medication for 40 days. We were in Bagerhat, the place of my maternal grandfather. After recovery, my parents decided to go to our place in Kotakole via Belphulia Ashram. I expressed to my mother that it would be nice if I get 'payesh' (a sweet condensed rice-milk product) in Ashram. After reaching Ashram we touched Baba's feet. I was then given 'payesh' to eat. The lady who cooked told, 'That day Baba advised her for making payesh'. In Konnagar Ashram also we have gone several times, but not before 1959/1960. And we left East Bengal in 1948 and we were in Ranaghat. I remember, twice we met him in the waiting hall in Ranaghat railway station along with many other disciples. Once he stayed for a night in our resident in Ranaghat. His blessings gave us hope and power to fight out the odds we faced after the partition of Bengal.

On 12.09.1959 he wrote a letter from Belphulia Ashram to a disciple which narrates the summary of our spiritual life:

'Mother, yesterday I received your letter dated 02.09.59. My health is now all right, but weak. This mortal body would *not be forever. Why are you worried for this? I am immortal and not to be conquered by death ('ajeya'). I have no birth, no death. I have no old age, no disease. The body has old age and disease. I am not the body. I am separate from the body. I am the inner self of the body. I am sole. The sole has no birth, no death and no old age. The sole is ever in existence. The sole is not destroyed. The sole has no deviation from its form. I have thus no deviation from my form, i.e., any change.*

Swami Dhyananda'.

Shri Shri 108 Swami Madhabananda Giri Maharaj

Shri Shri 108 Swami Madhabananda Giri Maharaj

We call him Thakur Baba, or, simply Baba. I came in his touch after my marriage in 1968, when his age was 238, yes, I mean 238. He was born in 1730. His full name is Shri Shri 108 Swami Madhabananda Giri Maharaj. He used to be called as Thakur Baba, or, simply Baba. He was also known as Mouni Baba, as he remained 'mouna' (silent without speaking any word) for the major part of his life. In 1960 he left his 'Mounabrata'. In 1820, when he was ninety years old, his Guru Bhagawan Ganguly handed over the charge of Thakur Baba and his friend Lokenath Baba (who was also a Great Saint) to Trailanga Swami in Varanasi, when he felt that he would leave his old body very soon. Trailanga Swami used to be called as "Living God". In the Varanasi Temple of Trailanga Swami, by the side of the Photo of Trailanga Swami there are still today five more photos of great saints under worship every day. One of them is of Thakur Baba (photo attached – source: Sankar Basu, Babugunj, Bakultala, District Hooghly, West Bengal, India).

The photo of Thakur Baba is the top left one in this temple of Trailanga Swami.

My mother-in-law and father-in-law were his disciples. In fact, her mother and father were his disciples. And that Guru-Sishya (Master-Disciple) relation came down to the successive generations. The parents of my mother-in-law lived in

Hooghly on the bank of the Ganges. An Ashram for Baba was built up on a big piece of land in Jagudas Para, Hooghly. The land was donated by a disciple. The old ashram of Baba was in Ujjain. But he never used to stay at any settlement for a long time. A major part of every year he used to be in the Himalayas. His disciples of the spiritual line used to be there. The rest of the time he used to be in Ujjain, Lucknow and Hooghly and in later part of life in Konnagar also, where another ashram was built up on the Ganges. He used to roam in order to guide his disciples who were scattered in different places. We do not have any idea of his disciples of spiritual line. They never came to any Ashram, or, in the residence of any domestic disciple. Perhaps, they were not allowed to mix up with the domestic disciples. Only two 'chelababa' (brahmachari disciple) used to accompany him on his visits to the domestic disciples, either in any ashram, or, in anyone's residence, where accommodation would be possible for him, chelababa, and other disciples accompanying him. Many eminent persons were his disciples. And there were many disciples from middle and low income group. His love and affection were there for everyone.

The history tells that in the year 1730, in the village of Chaurasi Chakla, also known as Kochua, two boys were born in two families. One was the child named Lokenath, the son of Ramnarayan Ghosal. The other was Benimadhab (our Thakur Baba) from the Bandyopadhyay family. Ramnarayan Ghosal was determined to depute a son to take the spiritual path to attain 'Moksha' (enlightenment). But he waited for his wife to hand over a son to him for this purpose. When Lokenath, the fourth son was born, she handed him to her husband to fulfill his desire. After Upanayan in 1741, Ramnarayan requested Acharya Bhagawan Ganguly, a Vedic scholar, to be his son's Guru (Master) to lead him to the path of 'Moksha'. Lokenath's childhood friend Benimadhab whose Upanayan was also performed in 1741, was bent upon going with Lokenath to attain the same objective. His family members could not resist him. Such was the spiritual urge and determination of such an eleven years old boy to take the path of religion to attain enlightenment. The two friends along with Guru Bhagawan Ganguly left the village and travelling a long distance by foot ultimately came to Kalighat near Calcutta (now Kolkata). At that time the place was in forest and was famous for the temple of Kalimata (Goddess Kali). The place was inhabited by saints, with long matted hair and wearing loincloth. The two friends Benimadhab and Lokenath felt at home in the place. Sometime they would disturb the sadhus by pulling their hair and the loincloth. One day Guru Bhagawan told them that they were also destined to lead a life of sanyasi like them. After knowing this, the two boys urged their Guru to leave that place and enter into the deeper forest in order to cut the link with their family members who used to come to Kalighat with money and food for them. They went inside the deeper forest and under the guidance of their Guru they started meditation along with practicing the Ashtanga Yoga of Patanjali and the most difficult Hatha Yoga. Along with the deep meditation they started practicing the fasting vows, starting for a day, then for two days up to twelve days at a stretch, then for a month at a stretch, without breaking their sitting postures. Guru Bhagawan took complete care of them, right from begging alms, preparing their food to even attending their call of nature.

After 12 years, as per the custom of sanyasi, Guru Bhagawan took them back to the place of their birth. The two young boys enjoyed their stay in the place of birth. Their age now comes to around 23. Guru Bhagawan patiently waited for them to reach that stage, when they would feel to come out of the worldly affection and pleasures. The day came very soon. The three holy men were again on the road sometime in 1753/1754 and headed for the heavenly abode of the Himalayas. There they practiced deeper meditation in bare body (nude state) for around 50 years. Finally they attained enlightenment in around 1804. They and their Guru Bhagawan were thrilled. But Thakur Baba and Baba Lokenath were sad for their Guru and said, 'Baba. You were busy in looking after us and in doing so you yourself could not go for enlightenment.' Guru Bhagawan said, 'No matter, my boys. In the next birth I would be your disciple to go for deeper meditation and enlightenment'.

The three of them headed for Mecca and Medina, wishing to study the Holy Koran under a competent teacher. They reached Kabul (Afghanistan) where they stayed some time with Mullasadi who was a great poet and a scholar on Koran. From Kabul they went to Mecca and then to Medina. On the way to Medina through the desert, they met an enlightened Fakir, Abdul Gaffur. Thakur Baba and Baba Lokenath had high praise for his Yogic attainment.

At this stage, Guru Bhagawan felt that it was time for him leaving the old body. They came back to Varanasi (Banaras/ Kashi). Here Guru Bhagawan handed over his disciples to the great saint Trailanga Swami, saying 'Baba. Look after my boys'. The age of the boys was ninety. It appears to be the year 1820. Guru Bhagawan left his body apparently in the year 1828, while in meditation at Manikarnika Ghat (rows of platforms from surface to a depth in the river).

After Guru Bhagawan passed away, Thakurbaba, Baba Lokenath and Trailanga Swami headed for the West, travelling through the various parts of Europe, Persia, Arab and Afghanistan. Mathematically, the tour to the West lasted for around 06 years, since they returned to the Himalayas possibly in the year 1834 at the age of 104 years. After getting accustomed with the climate after intense meditation for 03 years, they decided to follow the route taken by Pancha Pandav (as described in Mahabharata) during Maha-Prasthan (last journey). The three yogis travelled, starting in the year 1837, across the Himalayas to Mansarobar and then getting down to the Tibetan Plateau to Siberia to the Arctic Circle, what they described as the place of 'No Sun'/complete darkness. That means they went there in the mid-Winter, when the Sun was to the Southern Hemisphere. Here they stayed for a long period. Then they returned through China. In China, Trailanga Swami bed good bye to them and headed for his destination (possibly Varanasi) possibly in the year 1860. This indicates that their tour to Arctic Circle and back to China lasted for around 23 years. Thakur Baba and Baba Lokenath went to Chandranath Pahar (Hill) near Sitakunda in East Bengal (present Bangla Desh) possibly in the year 1862. It is a famous Shakti Peeth. As per Hindu sacred texts, the right arm of Goddess Shakti fell here. They stayed in the Chandranath Pahar for some time.

Here Baba Lokenath bed good bye to Thakurbaba possibly in the year 1863 and went to Daudkandi in Tripura, where he saved a person Dengu Karmakar from sure death. Dengu became his admirer and on his earnest request Baba Lokenath went with him to his native place Baradi in East Bengal in the year 1866 at the age of 136. He arranged for Baba's living in his house. After his death, the Nag family, the richest landlord of Baradi, built an Ashram for Baba Lokenath. Baba Lokenath became very famous and popular as a great enlightened saint and as a wise man not only in Baradi but in the whole of Bengal and beyond. In 1890, at the age of 160, Baba Lokenath left his body, while in meditation. Before leaving his body he made the following statement:

'I am eternal. I am deathless. After this body falls, do not think that everything will come to an end. I will leave in the hearts of all living beings in my subtle astral form. Whoever will seek my refuge, will always receive my grace'.

That is important – "whoever will seek my refuge", as Jesus said: "Behold, I stand at the door and knock. If anyone hears my voice and opens the door, I will come in to him and eat with him, and he with me."

From Chandranath Pahar, Thakur Baba went to Kamakshya for further meditation. From this time, the whereabouts of Thakurbaba were not known to the common people. His sanyasi disciples might know. After a long time Thakur Baba was found in an Ashram in Ujjain, a few kilometers from Ujjain Shiva Temple. That time it was a part of the forest by the side of Shipra Nadi, west of the Shiva Temple (I visited the Ujjain Ashram twice in 1990s, but only the abandoned Ashram building and premises, as Thakur Baba left his body long back).

Gradually his name and fame, as an 'Uchcha Kati Sadhu' (saint of high level of enlightenment), spread far and near. On earnest request of some disciples from Calcutta, Thakurbaba started coming to Calcutta at times so that his West Bengal disciples can meet him easily. Therefrom he came to Hooghly by request of some disciples. One disciple donated a large piece of land for his Ashram in Hooghly. The disciples volunteered themselves to build up the Ashram establishment. He used to come to Hooghly with two 'chelababa' (brahmachari disciples). Later on another Ashram was built in Konnagar on the river Hooghly (part of the Ganges). A part of the year he used to stay with his domestic disciples and part of the year in the Himalayas with his Sanyasi disciples. There was absolutely no link between the two groups of disciples. There were times when the domestic disciples accompanied him to Hardwar/Rishikesh/Kedarnath/ Badrinath/ Gangotri/Gomukh, but in those journeys no Sanyasi disciples were involved.

In one Kumbh mela, some of his domestic disciples saw him heading the Naga Group of Sadhus, sitting on the front elephant in the journey to take bath in the holy river.

I experienced some moments of his divine love and affection to every one coming to the Ashram to pay homage to him, irrespective of whether he/she is his disciple or not. I used to go with my wife Dipti and my mother-in-law (Namita; commonly known as Bubu) to have 'darshan' of Thakur Baba (to see Thakur Baba) in Hooghly Ashram and in Konnagar Ashram. But it was occasional, as my working place was in Rajasthan. This was the period from 1968 (year of my marriage) to 1974 (when Thakur Baba left his divine body).

Some photos of Thakur Baba are produced below. The source is Sankar Basu, Babugunj, Bakultala, P.O. & District Hooghly, West Bengal, India. He is cousin of my wife and a great devotee of Thakur Baba. He is the main person looking after the upkeep of the Hooghly Ashram of Thakur Baba and the various activities centering the Ashram.

Few More Photos
of Thakur Baba

A. At Younger Age

B. At Older Age

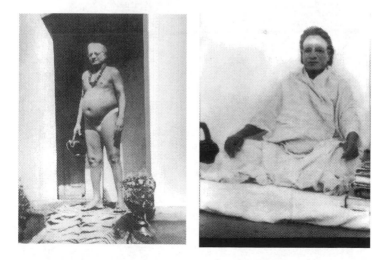

Some Remarkable Events with Thakur Baba

It is the experience of the people in India that the transcendental saints normally do not show the Divine Power they have attained. But at times, in need of the circumstances, the people see glimpses of their supernatural power. Of course, nothing is supernatural. Everybody is a part of God and has the Power sleeping in them. Under the present condition of our mind and body it cannot act. The common people like us would not be able to bear the manifestation of that power.

My mother-in-law, my wife, her Masi (mother's sister) and Dida (mother's mother) had the opportunity to witness the outcome of the divine power of Thakur Baba in 2/3 occasions only.

Occasion One

Once it happened in a day of his giving 'mantra' ('diksha') to some devotees. The ceremony of giving 'diksha' is used to be associated with worship and 'Homan' (giving sacrifices of ghee etc. to holy fire along with chanting of 'mantra'). That time, for want of a hall, the act of giving 'diksha' used to take place in open (under the sky). That day it was raining. The disciples were engaged in the room in taking stock of all the items required for 'homan', flower etc. But they were worried, as the rain was not stopping. They approached Thakur Baba what to do. He advised them to remain engaged in their job and not to worry. They finished their job. It was still raining. When the 'Lagna' (scheduled time for the diksha) approached, they had to approach Baba again, 'Baba. The Lagna would pass. How we can lit pious fire in the 'Homkunda' in the open under the rain and carry out the whole festival!' Baba came out in the open and with a stick made a rectangular spacious area on the ground. The rain stopped for a while. Quickly the things were arranged on the marked ground. The fire was lit and the worship started. The rain started again. Everywhere there was rain except the marked area. My wife and my mother-in-law were there, witnessing *this miraculous event. Otherwise it would be difficult for me to believe it.*

Occasion Two

Baba was fond of making afternoon ride along the Ganges in a car, accommodating as many disciples as possible. Once it happened that during the return journey the car stopped, as the Petrol was totally consumed. Baba at first rebuked the driver for his lack of responsibility. Baba was very particular for the duties to be carried out by individuals either at home or in the service. After a while Baba called the driver to take out the jerry can from the car's boot (dicky/trunk) and to bring water from the pond which could be seen from the car itself. Then he advised the driver to pour the water in the petrol tank. Behold! With that water the car engine started to operate. The driver drove the car back to Ashram. Then Baba told the driver to take out the water from the petrol tank and to give it back to the same pond wherefrom it was taken. My mother-in-law was a witness of this miraculous event.

Occasion Three

Once Baba came to the Hooghly Ashram with back pain. On enquiry it was found that Baba fell on ground, while in the Himalayas. He was not interested in any examination by any doctor. But the disciples went on insisting. A renowned doctor examined him and advised for x-ray of the backbone. Baba was taken to Calcutta by the doctor and the disciples. On seeing the x-ray plate the doctor got astonished. He saw the pictures of gods and goddesses like Rama, Krishna and Lakshmi on the image of the vertebral column. He rushed to the Hooghly Ashram with the x-ray plate and showed the image to the disciples. When Baba was asked about it, he simply said, 'How can I know? Can you see your back?' From that day the doctor became a great disciple of Baba. However, the x-ray plate did not show any major injury. And Baba got cured after a few days.

Occasion Four

The famous singer Nachiketa Ghosh (Senior Nachiketa) was Baba's disciple. One day Baba gave him 'Diksha', by writing mantra on a slate (that time Baba was under mounabrata – to remain *always in silence without uttering any word). After diksha it is customary to give some 'dakshina' (alms) to Guru (Master). Nachiketa was very poor and hesitating what to do. He said, 'Baba. With my condition what can I give to you?' Baba then pointed to the flowers offered to the Shiva Lingam and indicated by the fingers to take flower from the Shiva Lingam and place it on his feet. Nachiketa hesitated. After all, we cannot think of taking flower from a Shiva Lingam or, any other representation of God and put it on the feet of any human being. Baba's soul was in a human body. Then Baba indicated by the fingers, 'That Shiva Lingam would not be able to give you anything. This Shiva would give you whatever you want'. Such was his state of enlightenment. Jai Guru.*

Occasion Five

One time, before going to my place in Bhilwara in Rajasthan, I went to the Hooghly Ashram along with my wife and my mother-in-law to take his blessings. Before leaving, Baba told me, 'After boarding any vehicle, take Guru's name three times'. On that journey I reached Jaipur by train and from there in the next day I took our office jeep for the trip to Bhilwara – a distance of 250km. There were two young doctors and an engineer accompanying me; they were posted in Bhilwara. It was a left-hand-drive jeep. The two doctors were in the back seat. I and the Engineer were in the front seat (on the right-hand side). Around 30km before reaching Bhilwara, our vehicle was at the back of a truck. Suddenly our driver steered to the right to take over the truck. I saw a truck coming from the opposite side and shouted. But our driver did not notice my reaction. Our jeep dashed against the truck coming from the opposite side. Spontaneously we held the front rod tightly. The bonnet of our jeep was blown due to the impact and the front of the jeep went straight under the truck and stopped with a heavy jerk. The truck driver, after the initial shock, came down and rebuked our driver, saying, 'You fool. Had I not been able to dead-stop the truck before the collision, your bodies could not be traced.' What an escape! Mercy of Baba. Only the engineer, sitting on my right in the front seat, had minor injuries. Others did not have even a scratch. With God's blessings, the power of the Nature acted to save us. What would happen, if the truck could not be halted fully before the head-on collision! Guru is God and God is Guru. That is why an enlightened saint can say, 'sarba dharman parityajya mamekan smaranan braja' (leaving all the religions, meditate on me).

You receive His mercy more and more, the more you depend on Him and surrender to Him. At the super stage of enlightenment no difference exists between Guru and God. Perhaps an enlightened saint can realize and feel that he is nothing but a part of God, the Super consciousness. And at that stage of mind and soul, he automatically gets the power of God. And God's wish becomes his wish. He cannot misuse the power of God.

Occasion Six

There was no witness for this occasion. But we have complete faith in him and Lokenath Baba. This incidence shows how much love they had not only for the human being, but for the other lives on earth.

I narrated that on the return journey from the Arctic Circle via China, Thakur Baba and Baba Lokenath arrived in Chandranath Pahar (Hill) in Present Bangla Desh (that time it was in East Bengal in undivided India). They stayed in Chandranath Pahar for quite some time. They stayed in a Guha (cave). Close to the cave, they found a tigress along with a cub. The tigress never harmed them. This was a new born cub. For a few days, the tigress could not go for hunting, leaving the cub. Then she used to place the cub in front of the cave and went for hunting. After a few days, Thakur Baba and Lokenath Baba decided to leave the place. They left the place and started walking through the jungle. Then they heard a great roar. Looking back they saw the tigress was roaring looking at their departure from the place. They realized that the tigress wanted their presence for some time more till the cub was grown up further. They stayed there for a month. Such was there divine love for everyone.

Occasion Seven

My wife's Dida (maternal grandmother), Masi (maternal aunt) and her Mamato Bhai (son of her maternal uncle) were great disciples of Thakurbaba, especially her Dida whom Thakur Baba used to call as 'Dharmaraj' (king of religion – no gender considered). My wife's Dadu (maternal grandfather), i.e., husband of Dharmaraj was very worried at that time regarding their brickfield close to the river Ganges, as the river started breaking down the bank, approaching the brickfield, which was and still now is a major source of their income.

There are many such private brickfields along the river Ganges. The technique is that a short canal connects the river with a pond close by. During high tide in the monsoon season, the silt from the river enters the pond and gets settled on the tank's bed. After the monsoon is over, the connection of the tank with the river gets sealed. The water from the tank is taken out after the silt gets settled on the bed. Since the silt from the river is the source of brick-making, one cannot permanently seal the brickfield from the river; neither the brickfield can be taken away from the river.

One day, Dadu told his wife, 'everyday all the time you talk of Gurudev. Why don't you tell him of our hapless condition regarding the river approaching the brickfield by breaking off the bank at the canal? If this goes on, there will not be any brickfield to us in the near future'. His wife (Dharmaraj) hesitated in telling Baba about the domestic problems. In the Ashram, Baba used to talk about the different aspects of divinity and spirituality. After two/three days, Baba asked her, 'I am seeing that you are in deep anxiety for a few days and your mind is diverted. What has happened?' She told him of the brickfield problem. Then Baba said, 'Well. Take me a day to your brickfield'. Accordingly, Baba, along with a few disciples and my wife's Mama, Masi, Dadu and Dida (Dharmaraj) went to the brickfield. Baba stopped them much away from the river. He went alone to the riverbank, holding a stick. After a while, he returned and told them, 'I have drawn a line between the river and the brickfield. And I have told Ganga Mayee (Mother Ganga), if you cross this line, then either you would exist, or, I would exist'. About 50 years have passed since then (1965 to 2014). There is no further breaking of the bank of the river against the brickfield. There is no danger till today regarding the operation of the brickfield.

Fortunate to Receive Special

Blessing from Thakur Baba

I remember, once before going to my place of work in Bhilwara, Rajasthan, I was sitting along with others in front of Thakur Baba. That was sometime in 1973. Baba left his body in 1974 (we won't say, he left the world. We very much feel his spiritual presence with us).

My mother-in-law advised me to gently massage the legs of Baba. I was doing that. A time came, when for some work or other in the Ashram, others left the place gradually. I was the only person sitting with Baba, gently massaging his legs. In the mind, I was thinking, 'What to ask for from Baba. He would do whatever is good to me'. Suddenly Baba said, 'O.K. It would be done (Ja. Tor Habe)'. I was bewildered. He read my mind and blessed me.

That year onward, my service life and my personal life were on a better track, opening more opportunities for me. The top officials of GSI started giving recognition to my technical and administrative performance. Some points I summarize here in a nutshell:

1974: I submitted my final report on the Bhilwara Project, combining activities from 1970 to 1974. I was transferred back to my hometown Calcutta in the Coal Wing of GSI.

1975: I was shifted to the Technical Cell of the Director General, GSI. That year I was promoted to the post of Senior Geologist.

A number of responsibilities were ushered on me:

I represented GSI in CGPB (Central Geological Programming Board of the Government of India) Sub-committees on building up National Mineral Inventories for Copper-Nickel and Lead-Zinc during Fifth and Sixth Planning Commission, conducted by Indian Bureau of Mines.

I was given the charge of editing the Final Report of East Coast Bauxite of GSI and computing the reserve along with N. Bhaumick, Sr. Geologist. Because of my comments, dozens of plates of the report had to be redrawn by East Coast Bauxite Team, correcting the wrong extrapolations applied.

In 1980 I was selected in the High Level Joint Commission for mineral exploration between India and Russia and stayed in Russia (then USSR) for more than a month to finalize the document after paying visits to their mineral fields in Donetsk (Donbas) coal basin in Ukraine, Lebedinskoe iron ore near Belgorod, polymetallic porphyry deposit at Almalyk near Tashkent, polymetallic base metal deposits in Caucasus near Arkhonskoe, Kalmakir, Sarry Chikku etc. and the laboratories in Moscow, Leningrad, Ordzhonikidze, Rostov-on-Don, Tashkent, Samarkand etc.

I represented GSI in Hinterland Resource Management Committee for Paradeep Port under the Ministry of Surface and Water Transport.

The real game started after that. In 1991, I was promoted to the post of Director as a routine promotion as per seniority. I was selected for posting in the Coal Wing of GSI in Calcutta. But I had to pay the fees for sending technical letters on behalf of the Director General to the Regions under the Charge of Deputy Director Generals (DDG), two of whom were cross with me for modification of East Coast Bauxite Report and for pointing out the premature termination of drill hole without intersecting the interpreted existence of a footwall lead-zinc lode in Rajpura-Dariba belt of Rajasthan (later on it was proved by drilling). The DDG, Rajasthan became the Director General before my promotion to the post of Director. The third DDG was the DDG of Coal Wing itself, where I pointed out the wrong way the proved reserve used to be estimated for the coal reserve (which was changed after that).

So, instead of posting in Calcutta, I was suddenly posted to Raipur of Chhattisgarh, where nobody wanted to go, but the Director, staying then in Raipur, a favorite of the present Director General, was to come back to Calcutta.

This transfer upset me, but I did not try to cancel it. Ultimately this unwanted transfer became a boon to me. While I was in Raipur Office, Professor M.W. Khan, Head of the Geology Department, Pandit Ravi Shankar Shukla University sent a man to me who wanted to know whether the five pieces of mineral grains brought by him were diamond or not. I found the pieces to be uncut natural diamond. On enquiry he told that 03 pieces were from the Mainpur area of Raipur district and 02 pieces were from the Kunkuri area of Jashpur district. He did not mention the right spots. This prompted me to study the literatures and to pay visits to Mainpur and Kunkuri areas, discussing with local people and to study the geology and structure of the areas based on published and unpublished GSI maps and reports. Then, being confirmed for the presence of diamond in both the areas, I delineated the area for search of the primary source of diamond in both the areas. In 1992-93 field season the program for Mainpur area was taken up. As per advice of the Sr. DDG, Central Region the program was camouflaged: instead of writing 'search for the primary source of diamond' we mentioned 'search for the primary source *of precious and semi-precious stones' and a second program on search for ultra-pure silica was incorporated under the same item as a separate program. I put geologists Biplob Chatterjee and his wife Neeharika Jha, B.K. Mishra and others in execution of the program. Fortunately within three months the Bahradih and Payalikhand kimberlite pipes were detected. Both are not only diamondiferous, but also of mineable grade. Three more bodies were found subsequently – one in Kodomali area and two in Jangra area. My team received the National Mineral Award of the Government of India on this account based on my initial recommendation and further processing by the higher officials of GSI.*

I was made a member in the Scrutiny Committee for GSI programs on precious and semiprecious stones and on noble metals (because of my efforts in finding gold mineralization in the Kotri belt).

More than this I received in the last part of my stay in GSI and after my retirement from GSI. I was working as Director-in-Charge, GSI, Chhattisgarh since 1991. The date of my retirement was the 28th of February, 2002. I planned to retire from the services in Raipur itself instead of asking for a transfer to my hometown Calcutta as was customary. In 2000 I received a letter from the South Asian Association of Economic Geologists (SAAEG) requesting me to accept the Chairmanship of the Managing Committee for an International Seminar on Diamond and Kimberlites to be conducted by SAAEG in Raipur in July, 2001. I accepted. The preparations were going on. There was a good response, receiving around 200 papers from India and abroad. In May, 2001, due to some unavoidable reasons, it was decided to shift the date of the Seminar to February, 2002. In November, 2001 a representative from Jindal Steel and Power Limited (JSPL) came to me in order to know about the scope of exploration for diamond and kimberlite in India and abroad, saying that their Vice-Chairman-cum-Managing Director, Naveen Jindal (Chairman being his father Late O.P. Jindal) had taken interest in exploration for diamond after seeing the South African deposits. Knowing about the Seminar, JSPL made the maximum contribution to the Seminar fund along with De Beers and Rio Tinto.

On the Inauguration Day of the Seminar in February, 2002, Naveen Jindal along with V. Gujaral, CEO and Anand Goel, Director came to attend the inaugural function followed by the 1st day of paper presentation. Since it was the same month as that of my retirement, someone in the dais suggested for my more involvement in SAEEG activities after retirement on the 28th day of February, 2002. Knowing that I was retiring, Naveen Jindal advised V. Gujaral and Anand Goel to contact me for my services as a consultant in JSPL for exploration in diamond and kimberlites. See the coincidence:

Had

1. Naveen Jindal not taken any interest in exploration for diamond (which has no connection at all for their core business of Steel and Power Plants) after seeing the diamond mine in South Africa,
2. The seminar date not shifted to February, 2002, the month of my retirement from GSI,
3. Naveen Jindal not come to attend the Inauguration of the Seminar in February, 2002,

my selection as a Consultant in JSPL would not materialize. This is not a big thing to many persons. But, at my financial condition, this shelter was a great thing to me and I am grateful to Naveenji (to show respect to a person we suffix 'ji' after the name) for that.

I told them that there was one per cent chance in getting a mineable diamondiferous kimberlite, as in the World there were around 7000 kimberlites out of which around 700 are diamondiferous and around 70 are mineable. But Naveen Jindal did not hesitate to take decision to go ahead.

It solved my financial need after retirement from GSI, as I could not save much funds before retirement because of other commitments.

All these, I believe, are the effect of blessings from Thakur Baba. My future got stability and I could perform my family duties and social duties in a better way. Till today I am working as a Consultant in JSPL at the age of 73. This was possible, as God kept me and my wife free from any major ailments.

I wonder, Naveenji's strong Will for taking part in exploration for diamond and his Patience in this respect and my need for a good job – did Nature conspire, under God's Grace, to bring it together? Well, I am benefited, no doubt.

But what about Naveenji? Would he be able to get a mineable diamondiferous kimberlite pipe? Under allowance from

Naveenji and Goel Sahab, I have been able to set a capable team of Geologist and Geophysicist and a small, but efficient, Laboratory in this purpose. We have found a cluster of kimberlites in Gumla district of Jharkhand with a lot of G3 (eclogitic) and G4 (pyroxenitic) garnets, the major part being G3D and G4D (coming from diamond bearing eclogite and pyroxenite layers of the mantle). Now we are heading for microdiamond testing of the selected drill cores. Similarly, we have located around 16 anomalous blocks in Jashpur district of Chhattisgarh based on kimberlite indicator mineral, each block already narrowed down to less than a square-kilometre to around 4.00 sq.km. We are to carry out test drilling in these blocks to locate concealed kimberlites. We may mention here that our report is the only report of the presence of kimberlite in Jharkhand. Except our team, no other teams including GSI and NMDC have found the presence of any kimberlite in Jharkhand.

I pray to my Guru for giving us at least one mineable diamondiferous kimberlite for Naveenji as a response to his patience in this respect and our sincere and honest efforts in search for a mineable diamondiferous kimberlite.

Religion and Science/
God and Mother Energy

I am a student of science. I am a religious person having faith in God. As a Layman I do not find any difficulty in thinking together of Science and God. If the Engineers and Scientists can create some products out of matter and energy, then why not God can create the Universe scientifically taking help of Mother Energy associated with Him, the Super consciousness? The scientists would say, 'Is it necessary to bring God to create the Universe, when Mother Energy can perform to create the Universe?' Well, when the scientists want to make a product, can matter and energy perform on their own to create the product without intervention of the scientist to guide it in the same line in an orderly way? The Universe exists in an orderly way, indicating some Super brain *behind it. It is not a haphazard formation. Moreover, there are many unpredictable equations in life, like prediction of future by enlightened saints, their control over Nature, their reading of other's thinking without the help of any instrument... etc. These cannot be explained by the science of matter and energy, but the observations cannot be denied. There must be some Entity whose power can do all these things and the enlightened saints get that power from Him.*

Physics to understand Universe

I read the copy of a lecture delivered by Professor Michio Kaku of Cuny (The City University of New York), USA. He has rightly said, 'Physics is at the very foundation of matter and energy'. But it is not the foundation to understand Consciousness. Has energy a brain, or, Will Power to act as per its liking/disliking/ whims? No. But man can do it, using the same energy in one or other form. There is some entity beyond matter and energy to guide them to act, following the universal laws set by him. There might be some other type of matter, different from present state of matter and anti-matter in the present Universe, in some extinct Universe, or some Universe to come after the extinct of the present Universe, which would follow some other types of universal laws set by the Omnipresent Almighty.

Kaku said, 'In my life I've had two great passions. First is to help complete Einstein's dream of a theory of everything. An equation one inch long that would allow us to "Read the mind of God". But the second passion of my life is to see the future'.

With progressive science, opening petals of Applied Knowledge, we may attain a higher level of understanding of scientific codes and produce many gadgets enabling a different way of living on earth or somewhere in outer space. We may attain a higher level of understanding where we would be able to read each other's mind and thoughts, by understanding the electromagnetic codes produced by the thoughts. The same can be done today by the enlightened saints. They can also perceive, if they want, the future events to be taken place in a man's life. There are many witnesses, to such acts of them. This type of reading by the saints is beyond the skill of any scientific development.

'There are many things, Horatio than are dreamt of in your philosophy'.

This is beyond any level of knowledge of matter and energy. We cannot deny their power of predictions on any 'going to be accident', or, death for an apparently healthy person. Many such cases are in human history. We should not deny, or, ignore those. Rather, we should try to understand how it happens. It is not like the physical coding of DNA for the life structure, as it would be from a seed or, egg cell to a completely grown individual. If someone can tell of the main episodes of my future, it means that the future path of our life is coded – a coding which is beyond the natural power (energy) to understand. How is it coded, where is it coded and how to understand that coding? Is it a game played by God, using parts of Him (us) as pawns (since He is the only Entity)? The game is created by Him, played by Him and it is within Him.

The Enlightened Saints can predict the length of life of a person and about the main events going to take place in his life and the approximate time for such events. Perhaps, they also cannot predict the future of the Universe – how long it will expand, when to collapse, what will happen after that, what the different episodes are going on in different parts of the Universe etc. These are only known to the Creator. Call Him God or by any other name. Do not ignore His Consciousness. Matter and Energy are not conscious. They act as per will and action of someone conscious.

I have already mentioned the topic of this book as a Layman's thought. I may be right at certain points, or, wrong at certain points. But the Supernatural activities cannot be denied. We call them supernatural, as under our knowledge system cannot explain them.

Einstein's equation $E=mc^2$ and Sir Isaac Newton's $F=ma$ and Faraday's laws of electricity gave the scientists big jumps to understand the laws of motion, and the energy-matter relation. The scientists have understood the Four Forces played in the Universe – Gravity, Electromagnetic Force, Weak Nuclear Force and Strong Nuclear Force. The scientists understand the basic behavior of these forces – how they act. Can anybody understand why they act in that fashion? Why a mass attracts the other mass? Why are there positive and negative charges? What is actually magnetism? Why do the Forces behave in the way they are behaving?

These questions prick me – the mind and brain of a layman. The scientists have shown the way to take help of these forces *in making the products, or, in trying to understand the different events of the Universe. But can they, or, will they be able to create a new type of Force which will follow some other laws not known in the present Universe?*

The scientists have understood the conservation of energy that energy can neither be created nor can be destroyed. So, energy just exists and thus it has no beginning and no end. They are now trying to find out the mother form of the energy which just exists and from which the Universe has been formed. Has the so called Mother Energy a Mind to wish to create something in a planned way? Has the Mother Energy a mind to create intelligent life through evolution from a single cell to a complicated system of brainy human being? If there is no mind or consciousness behind any creation, then the accidental short term creation would be short-lived, because the creator would not be determined to act in a particular direction for a long time to have a planned creation step by step starting from a simple profile to a complex profile.

This is the major difference between religious thoughts and scientific thoughts.

Our mind understands something which has boundaries – particular time, particular distance, beginning and end; it cannot understand "no time" state, no beginning state, no end state, no boundary in space, never ending space. We are born in a certain environment, having limitations and thus unable to perceive the state beyond any limitation. We can deal with matter and energy, but we cannot go beyond that – to perceive Super consciousness. That is the limitation of present scientific procedures. But the Science being cultured by the Enlightened Saints go beyond matter and energy to realize the hands of God, the Creator – the Super consciousness, Energy being His hands. If your mind can attain the state of 'no thought, no vibration', it may feel that state, or, at that state of mind, the unknown gets reflected – the unknown who will never be understood through science of matter and energy, even if we can discover the Mother Energy of all energies. We are to realize the Mother Consciousness of all conscious nesses, i.e., the Super consciousness.

If Mother Energy is just Energy without any Sense like Wish, Will, Planning, Coding, then how Mother Energy without any sense imposes strict law and order in not only forming the Universe, but maintaining it? Does the extent of the Universe is the extent of Mother Energy, or, Mother Energy occupies the limitless Space. When some entity becomes limitless, it has to be static. The only difference between Religion and Science is that Religion believes in Super consciousness with inseparable Mother Energy as the Ultimate Entity and Science believes only in Mother Energy as the Ultimate Entity.

God, Space and Time

Many unexpected little things happen in life. Are they just accidental? Or, are they kind jokes of God who perhaps cherish these events bearing his blessings and our disbelief in his hands in such events? After all, God, the only entity covering the Universe and beyond, must be feeling boring to be alone and he then created the material universe out of him (God – an entity of Super consciousness and Mother Energy). In that way God is everywhere and we are within God. If God is everywhere, then God is also within us and we are within God. By God, if scientists believe only in Mother Energy, then we are to say Mother Energy is within us and we are within Mother Energy. This was expressed very nicely by Thakur (Reverend) Ramkrishna Paramhansa Dev that if we immerse a pitcher within a tank, or, a lake, water like God is within the pitcher and also outside the pitcher. The pitcher is like our body, the physical existence. When you can break the body, inside water (consciousness) unites with the vast outside water (Super consciousness). This is Liberation. It does not mean that the moment you leave your body on earth, you immediately gets united with God, the Super consciousness. You are leaving your coarse physical body, but staying with your finer body of your desires, ambition, good thoughts and bad thoughts.

So long the different desires are there in our mind, the Influence Zone of desires is strong enough not to allow us, the Consciousness to get liberated from the engulfment of desires and we cannot be liberated. This is what the Enlightened Saints say. This is the reason of the cycles of life and death and rebirth in this physical world. As if, the influence of the desires on us, the Consciousness acts like the Influence of Gravity for celestial bodies, where you cannot leave the celestial body before attaining the optimum speed to get out of the Influence Zone of the celestial body.

The Scientists believe that life is nothing but the physical bodies of the animal and plant kingdom. Naturally, *according to them, life ends with the death of the physical body. It is just a part of the biochemical process and nothing else. When life ends, the question of rebirth also is not there.*

Bertrand Russell, a great philosopher and an atheist (no faith in the existence of God) of the 20th century, was desperate to comment under great philosophical disappointment that the man's origin, his growth, his feelings etc. are nothing but "the outcome of accidental collocations of atoms". All the human activities with its civilization, built up through ages, are going to extinct with the death of the solar system. No philosophy can reject them.

This great disappointment about life comes, when one does not believe of any existence beyond matter and energy, when one has no faith in the existence of Super consciousness.

Unfortunately, Bertrand Russell did not take pains to see/examine the other side of the coin. There were and still are many enlightened saints who can perceive the existence of soul after the death of the physical body - the liberated souls and the souls engulfed/captivated in the cover of desires. Thakur Ramkrishna used to talk with God, whom he worshiped in the form of Kali Mata (Mother Kali). This talk is not through the mouth of the idol of Kali Mata. He used to sense her part of the conversation mentally; this may be a play of the electromagnetic forces taking part in the conversation. The same was the case with Trailanga Swami of Banaras in India. When God is everywhere, you can worship anything in the name of God, assuming the presence of God in that object. And if your faith and devotion to God is very strong, you can feel the presence of God in the idol you are worshiping as God.

Here I mention again the words from the mouth of the Great Saint, Baba Lokenath:

'I am eternal. I am deathless. After this body falls, do not think that everything will come to an end. I will leave in the hearts of all living beings in my subtle astral form. Whoever will seek my refuge, will always receive my grace'. In the enlightened stage of realization, one does not feel that he is separate from God. He realizes that he is an integral part of God, as we feel that our hands and feet and the head are integral parts of our body. The only difference is that the parts of our body are different from each other, having different functions, but the souls, enlightened or not, are an integral part of God, the Super consciousness and there is no difference between the souls except that the enlightened souls are liberated from the binding of desires and can perceive and realize that they are nothing but an integral part of God, the Super consciousness.

Only after leaving all the desires, except the only desire to unite with God, you can attain the stage of Liberation.

Perhaps, we as Consciousness (part of Super consciousness) get absorbed in the psycho-matter combination of the body (including the invisible finer body of desires) and then we lose the realization that we are part of Super consciousness, because there cannot be any existence other than that which was from the Beginning and which has no Beginning.

This is like this. We know that something is formed out of something else. There cannot be any creation out of Nothing. That is why there is conservation of mass and energy combined together. When anything cannot be created from Nothing, there ought to be some entity in existence which had no Beginning. The problem is that we can understand the logic behind it, but we cannot realize it.

The scientists think that the present Universe was formed out of Big Bang of a nuclear entity and so the Universe had a beginning. The saints also said that the Universe was formed through 'Omkar Dhani' (sound of 'Om', the vibration). Both conceive the same event that at a time the Universe was formed and the matter exists only through movements/vibrations. Up to this is o.k. But what was that some entity from which the Universe was formed? There ought to be something which has no beginning, just exists and there is no end. The present Universe may end, or, wind up completely from its present expanding stage. It may go back to that eternal entity which is in existence, having no beginning. You can call that entity as God, or, the Creator who just exists, no beginning, no end and no spatial limit of the existence. The Universe is within Him, the Creator. It may happen that the present Universe has formed as per His coding and would last till the fulfillment of the coding.

Many scientists remark that when the Universe is formed by the Mother Force of the Nature, why is it necessary to bring God as a Creator. They would say that the present expanding stage of the Universe is after Bing Bang and there was another stage of the Universe before the Bing Bang. This means that these are the different cycles of the Universe which had no beginning; only, it is changing its form in different cycles. Where is the place of God in that? Well, the expanding Universe at any point of time has a limit, occupying a part of the Space. It cannot be a Creator itself for all the manifestations in the endless Space. Then following the Scientists' idea, we are to assume that there would be then millions of Universes occupying parts of the never-ending Space. And these Universes would have no connection with each other, but they are keeping a distance between them, avoiding any clash. And all the Universes are a product of matter and energy and nothing else. Who is then maintaining this order of the Universes? Who has imposed the behavior of the different forces as they are behaving? Why there is Gravity that one mass attracts another mass? Why is there magnetic attraction? We know that under such physical/ physicochemical conditions, the reaction would be in this line. But who imposed such behavior in Energy. There may be other Universes, where the nature and behavior of Energy would be completely different, not following the physical rules of $F = ma$ and $E = mc^2$. The very existence of proton, neutron and electron may not be there. It is quite likely that there is

Some Entity who is planning these Games, occupying the never-ending Space. And if we overlay the findings/realization of the Enlightened Saints on the Scientist's Observations, we are to assume that there is Some Entity who is playing these Games within His astral Form – call Him (there is no gender for Him) God, or, Super consciousness. He is occupying the never ending Space and all the activities and phenomena are within Him. Let us discuss this assumption of God occupying the never-ending Space.

The question comes that if that God (Super consciousness with inseparable Mother Energy) is in existence without any beginning, what space (how much space) that Entity is occupying. If we say that He is occupying that much of space, then what is after that?

First we are to understand the Space itself. Is there any limit of the Space? If we say that an Entity occupies that much of Space, then what is after that? If nothing is there, that means empty space. If some other feature is there, that means that is occupying space and thus Space continues. Logically we are to say then that Space is limitless, never ending. Mathematically we may coin the term 'Infinity' for the limitless space, without understanding what it is. Can we put a Stop to Space, saying that beyond this point Space does not continue? If we assume that Space is spherical with a limit to the Sphere and if we move in a direction on the outer limit, we would come back to the same place of start, then also the question remains: what is after that spherical limit? The question 'what is after that?' will never die, unless we assume that Space is limitless. Our brain, as a part of the materialistic world, cannot conceive it.

If the Space is never ending, it has to be static. Is God totally occupying the never ending space and is static like Space? Hindu Saints, right from Vedic Age, has told that God is 'Anadi Anantam', i.e., NO beginning, No end (no end by virtue of time and no end by virtue of extent).

The next question comes of Time. God who has no Beginning and no End, there is no time for formation and no time for any end. The existence becomes timeless. It just exists. Time becomes meaningless. Saints try to feel this timeless affair through 'Dhyan-Dharana-Samadhi' (concentration to a particular idea or image, holding that idea/image in mind and getting absorbed totally in that idea/ image, when mind stops thinking) and the meditation becomes timeless. Time is a relative term of change of events within God, the Super consciousness-cum-Mother Energy. On the broad canvas, time has no meaning.

Does God know who he is, what he is? How? He is the only existence, without Beginning and End and without having any Father, or, Mother. He just exists. Who is He? He would perhaps say, 'I am the only Existence, covering endless Space and thus I am also endless. I have no Form, no Shape. Every form, every shape has to be limited. The word size has no meaning for me. The word time has no meaning for me, as there is no start or end for me. Yes, there are local changes in my shapeless formless body like there are boils, black spots, swellings, burns in your body, but that does not change my shapeless existence.'

Another issue has developed in my mind. If God/Super consciousness is occupying the whole of never ending Space, then a doubt appears regarding the existence of Space itself. We can simply say that there is nothing like Space. It is the never ending spread of God/ Super consciousness. All the phenomena, including the expanding Universe, are played within Him, occupying part of Him.

If God/Super consciousness is in never ending extent, then God is static, but is likely to be a vibrating medium. During concentration of mind on the openness in front of me under dim light, I have seen as if the openness is vibrating. I cannot see anything except the feeling of vibration. If anything vibrates very rapidly in front of your eyes, you will see it as a static object, but a feeling of vibration may occur in you. If such rapid vibration occurs in the rarest of rare medium, you will not feel its impact on your physical body, as we do not feel impact of light on our body, though it impacts our body with great speed. Again, I look at the openness in front of me under the Sun, but not the Sun rays hitting the eyes, I have seen as if the openness has a network of white patches and black threads, like a spider's net. I do not know whether these are just the play of my eyes, or, there is something in it. I request you all to try to concentrate in the same way in openness in front of you and find whether you are also experiencing the same phenomena.

For the peace of mind of us, the common people, it is better to surrender to God (Super consciousness-cum-Mother Energy) blindly than to try to get an answer of all these questions. That is what the most intelligent people, the True Saints, are doing. They thus attend a peaceful state of mind, surrendering everything to God – no desire of their own except the earnest desire to perceive His presence, to get absorbed in Him. From their life we may presume that if the state of mind becomes desire less except the only desire to realize the presence of God, the sole becomes pure. Almighty Himself then reveals His presence to him. He then realizes that he is also the same Super consciousness, occupying every part of Space. As we feel the touch on any part of our body, so also he can feel any event taking place, or, destined to take place in future, at least where he is concerned regarding the welfare of his close group. There must be a limitation of perceiving what is happening or going to happen, when the sole lives within the body, even if it is enlightened.

Lastly I am to say, there is no harm if the Scientists do not believe in God. They do believe in Mother Energy from which the other forms of energy have been formed. In that case, the physical bodies of the Scientists, which have formed ultimately from Mother Energy, become the off springs of Mother Energy. So, the Scientists can call her as Mother. Then, if Mother Energy is not having any Consciousness, the Scientists also then would have no Consciousness.

They only live who live for others / Love thy neighbor as thyself

These great advices should be a part of our life. The first advice is from Swami Vivekananda, the Great Disciple of Thakur Ramkrishna Paramhansa Dev and a Great Social Reformer, an Enlightened Saint himself and the Founder of Ramkrishna Mission. His life was dedicated for the welfare of the human being, for the welfare of the Society. He felt the necessity for these seven words – they only live who live for others. Today Ramkrishna Mission has hundreds of centers in India and in other parts of the world. Its main roles are spread of education, health care, upliftment of the societies, and moral and spiritual upliftments.

The second advice was a well-known old advice. This is from the Bible, uttered by Jesus Christ. The inner meaning of both the advices is the same. Extend your helping hands to others.

These summons should be a part of our life. To feel the desire to serve for others in their need, you are to love others. Start first loving your family members, following the proverb, charity should begin at home. Then spread love to other relations and friends. Gradually love will be an essential part of your life and you would start loving others who are not related to you, even the other creations of Nature. You would feel for your neighbors and for your society members. This was the culture in good old days, when people were aware of what was happening in their neighborhood; whether the neighbors were okay, whether they were financially able enough to arrange for their daily food. There were many drawbacks in those feudal societies, but neighbor to neighbor relation was there. Now a day we do not think for others except our few close intimates, especially in the multistoried residential complexes. Our Vedas say that one-fourth of our earning should be spent for helping others. That may not be possible for modern way of life, where even the expenditures towards education and medical treatments are exorbitant, becoming money-making centers. But at least a part of our earning should go for helping others as per our financial status.

We eat in hotels and restaurants, where many times we leave the excess food ordered beyond our capacity to eat. The management puts the left out food in the garbage bin. But this is good food, not the balance left on our dishes, but the excess food remaining in the serving containers. It pinches, when such good food is thrown in the garbage can for rotting. There should be some system adopted by the management to supply the good excess food to the needy/starving persons in the nearby localities. In most of the developing countries, there are many poor dwelling units, or, many persons living on the footpaths near the posh localities with hotels and restaurants. The excess food may be supplied there on a regular basis. I am sure, there would be many takers, if one supplies the good food with due respect to them.

Even in the developing and poor countries, there are many clubs – football clubs, cricket clubs, festival clubs (e.g., annual festivals of different kinds) etc. These clubs should come forward to act as helping hands for the welfare of the needy *people of the locality. If they approach the residents of the locality for this purpose, no body, baring few, will mind in giving contributions in this respect. These clubs can also arrange for cleanliness of the localities, through the efforts of the residents and through the vigilance of the designated employees engaged by the Government authorities for this purpose, just to see that they perform their duties properly.*

They only live who live for others. They do not live for others just for the sake of their welfare. They get pleasure in living for others. Once you experience this pleasure in your life, you will remain busy in extending your helping hands for others. It is not necessary that you sacrifice your life for helping others. Neither it is advisable, since you should also fulfill your duties towards your families and towards your commitments. In the midst of all these duties, you can try to help others, however small that help may be. What looks small for you may be a great help to the needy person in the time of his dire necessity.

I remember, in the first two years of 1980s my financial position was very tight. There were months, when I had to take a loan of Rs. 20/30 from any of my friends on the last days of the month just to purchase the daily needs. That help of Rs. 20/30 was a great help to me. Before taking the loan, I could not tell my friend that I needed that much money to purchase my daily needs, having no cash in my pocket. I pretended that I needed some changes, while going out of his house after gossiping for an hour or two. Next month, after getting the salary I returned that money.

So, I realized the importance of that advice – they only live who live for others.

Do not remain indifferent at least to the persons known to you. Indifference makes one lock up his mind against other's problems and that is a bad sign for the society. Not only for the society, for their own family also, where, for the lack of proper communications and openness of mind, the distance will grow between the family members. And happiness disappears. Life becomes a routine/ mechanical episode.

Prayer

Prayer is the best elixir for life. Though I am a Hindu, right from my boyhood days, I used to go to the Roman Catholic Church in Krishna Nagar to spend some time in that silent, soothing, cozy and serene environment of the Prayer Hall. There I noticed that a Nun always used to be on prayer, kneeling down in front of an idol of Jesus Christ, not in the main Hall, but in a side room separated from the main hall by a curtain. There was no bar in silently visiting that room. At intervals, the nun used to be replaced by another nun, but the prayer continued. This influenced me. And growing up I learnt about the strength of prayer from the holy books.

A fear cropped up in me in 1960, when I was in B.Sc. with Honors in Geology. My father was not well. I could not think of losing my father that early. It was not the question of only financial set-back. It was the question of losing beloved father and a beloved guardian. It clicked in my mind to take help of prayers. I started praying every day to God, asking for life of my father at least for another 10 years. I continued the prayer for years, by just modifying my language, for life of my father for at least 10 years from the day of my first prayer in this respect. My father died in 1970. That startled me. Just 10 years have passed and my father was no more! God then listened to my prayer and admitted it. He is so kind! Listening to the prayer of an ordinary man, not spiritually high!

From that time of 1970, I had no other choice but to remain ever grateful to God. And this event added strength to my faith in God. With such events, the root of your faith becomes stronger. And with stronger faith your mind gets more and more stability, becomes peaceful and cool, knowing that Some One is there to take care of you, if you are on the right track. If He is ready to give you, you are also to be ready (capable) to receive it. Righteousness is a strong quality to lead a good life. But as a common man, we cannot stick to righteousness always. Pray to God to take you out of your problems. At the same time you are also to work hard to come out of your problems. You will find that at times you fail even to solve a simpler problem. At times you come out of greater problems at ease. This depends on the Space-Time functioning on you. Praying to God would help you to reduce the intensity of the problem so that you can endure it, or, your bad Space-Time environ would change quickly. With your prayer add also something like this: 'God, I am a weak person. I am not right always in my duties. But I try to be good – good in my family duties, good in my office duties, good in my relation with my dear ones, friends and neighbors, good in not hurting my parents, my spouse and kids, good in not hurting my uncles and aunts, even we get separated mentally and physically, having some harsh stages in life. But there are faulty moments when I forget all the good human qualities. Forgive me and make my mind stronger in accepting righteousness more and more. Oh God, if needed be, punish me to put me on the right track, but let there be your mercy and love for me'.

After the death of my father, I stopped praying, as my only prayer was centered to my father. But prayer embossed its seal in my mind. After a long gap, I started praying again. I started praying for the welfare of my family members. Then it got extended to my close relations and a friend. The decades have passed. I have not stopped praying for them. My parents and my wife's parents are no more, but I pray for the welfare for their sole, be it free or gone in rebirth. My prayer got extended for the new members in the extended relations, first for my son-in-law and then for my daughter-in-law and to the son of my daughter Ruchira and the daughter of my son Shuvadeep. And the same also stands for other members in close relation.

I do not know how much it acts on the welfare of those for whom I am praying. But it keeps my mind happy that I am thinking for them every day.

I have narrated this for you to think on this line. Many of you must be doing this like me. Others are advised to follow. At least your mind would open for others. This is good for the social bondage. And it is good for you that you would not envy others by seeing their welfare. Your mind would remain peaceful.

I remember one incidence. Just a month before my father's death, I was in home in Calcutta (that time I was posted in Rajasthan). One noon after lunch, I was lying by the side of my father, putting my head on his chest. He suddenly told me, 'Khokon (My Child), Father does not remain forever. Take it easy. Life is like that'. I was in that position for a long time and when I got up, as if my body got totally embossed by his touch. Still I feel that feeling.

Two days before his death, he got the cerebral attack.

Father was admitted in Nilratan Sarkar Medical College and Hospital, where my brother Mihir was in internship after completing MBBS. The situation was critical. Seeing the condition, next morning my wife rushed to Thakur Baba in Hooghly to get his blessings for cure of our father. That morning Thakur Baba did not open the door of his room. My wife understood that the inevitable had come. She returned to Calcutta.

In 1971 our daughter Ruchira was born. In 1979, our son Shuvadeep was born. In his very infant days, some physical behaviors of Shuvadeep were very similar to those behaviors of my father. The way he used to cough was exactly the same as that of my father. And the movement of the head and the eyes in response to some talks (when he was around three years old) were exactly alike. I do not know whether it was the rebirth of my father. However, these qualities did not persist with grown up Shuvadeep.

Gratitude

Gratitude is a good quality in our life. With more and more commercial attitude people are forgetting, or, ignoring to remain grateful to those who helped them some time or other in their life. Their good gestures should be acknowledged by us, not just by the word 'Thanks', but by remaining grateful to them.

When we were in dire necessity of getting a boost in life and fortunately we get it through someone's help, or, the circumstances tuned in our favor, we forget it very soon. As a result we forget to remain grateful to that person but for his help, or, suggestions, we won't be what we are today. And we do not bother to remain grateful to God whose Will and Blessings created the circumstances in our favor and changed our life from zero opportunity to someone established in the Society. Even leading a life without any major illness for self and the family members is a great thing for which we should remain grateful to God. We should think that we are much better compared to so many people in more distressed conditions. We may not be highly placed, but we are leading a life without many disturbances and we could remain honest in our approach.

While worshiping any god, or, goddess, we invite Him/Her (of course, there is actually no gender for God; we love to imagine Him under different images) through mantras (special hymns), then offer a seat (asan), cloth, food and water and then pray for our welfare, asking for wealth, prosperity, education, fame, beauty etc., but there is no mantra to show our gratitude to God for what we have received already from Him. That is unfortunate.

Too much selfishness does not pay. And do not adopt Narcissism.

Spread your life on the bed of Gratitude so that you get a good sleep.

Balance

Human life in essential is a game of balance. It is absolutely different from the other forms of life of the animal and plant kingdoms. The supremacy of human life lies in its commitments and the moral and social duties. The duties and general activities are of many types and the full inclination to one side may neglect the other side. That is why the question comes of keeping the balance.

It is quite a difficult job to do justice to all the bindings and be a perfect man. It is practically not possible. But we should have the mind to try for it as much as possible. This is possible when we develop the attitude for this game of balance in life. With the positive attitude the success comes when the balance is maintained. I am presenting a simple and common example. A young married person is to look after the wife and children on the one hand and the dependent parents on the other hand and may be for unmarried sister and dependent brother. Do we always do it, keeping a balance? When the answer is yes, it is fine. But in most of the larger families (with more members than just a couple and their children), the common answer is no. The man in the center who is managing the house has failed to keep the balance. As a result the happiness and calmness evades from such houses. Of course, along with the man at the center, the other members should also play their role in a responsible way, having regard to the family bondage and love and regards to every member, no matter whether he/she is a senior or a junior. The balancing is more important and at the same time more difficult in the larger families of husband, wife, parents, children, sisters and brothers, as is the case in the Asiatic countries. If the members fail to keep the balance, it is wise for the parents and their son with wife and children to plan to live separately, but close by, so that at the time of any need, one can extend his helping hands to the other. In that way the relation will not be destroyed.

There are many chapters of balancing in life. The first chapter is to keep the balance between the attitudes of husband and wife towards each other. This is most important, as the center of management in a house lies with them. The husband and the wife have come from different families having their own ways of living. Their thinking and attitude towards family and social responsibilities may not be similar. Some families may be more self-centered and some are not. Some have been brought up in a larger undivided family keeping closeness to so many members. Some have been brought up in such families who keep a distance from the other relations. The husband and the wife may be from such families of different attitudes, but they should think that now they are together to enjoy a decent life, making their home a place of serene environment. In achieving such a loving environment, there is no harm in curtailing some personal likings and disliking by both the members, of course keeping the attitude of righteousness. If one puts a wrong step in the family matters, the other partner patiently should try to make him/her understand the wrong doings. If the husband and the wife have patience, soft corner, love and respect for each other, it will not be difficult to adjust. But no one should try to force the other member to accept some wrong moves. In the long run they may break the warm relation.

The second chapter of balancing lies between the daughter-in-law and her parents-in-law and between the son-in-law and his parents-in-law. In the countries like India, where after marriage the wife comes to live with husband and her parents-in-law (and unmarried sister and brother, if any), the balancing in attitude between the daughter-in-law and the parents-in-law (especially mother-in-law) is more important. There should have great patience from each side and love and respect for all. The parents-in-law should come forward to treat her as a beloved daughter who has left her sweet home and has come to live with the parents-in-law. The daughter-in-law should also have eagerness to change some of her habits which are not well taken in the changed environment. She should accept the good rules and regulations of the in-law's house. If something appears to be outdated, she should discuss it first with her husband, or, with the mother-in-law, if she is in her favor. Then it may be opened to all with a solution. In a cordial environment any practical suggestion is generally accepted by all the members. Happiness will exist under such circumstances.

The third balance in a family is the balance between the work schedule and the leisure period. A leisure time is required in the house when all the members assemble together to enjoy their relation. In these busy days the family get-together may be planned either during the morning tea session, or, on the dinner table, or, after dinner for half an hour, depending on the time schedule of the persons in service and the students having coaching classes. Such planned leisure is good not only to maintain the serene atmosphere, but also to reduce the everyday stress. We should work hard in our business, or, as an employee in an organization, but that is not our whole life. It is not at all advisable to work from morning to night, and then come back to home, take dinner and go to slip. This is no life.

The fourth balance lies in maintaining a balanced relation with friends and other relations like the families of brothers, sisters, uncles, aunts etc. This is the inner circle of the society around our family. This bondage would give confidence that during the time of need there are my friends and relations to assist me. And during the time of any celebration in our house they would eagerly come to make the atmosphere more pleasant. In keeping these relations, occasionally we should pay a visit to their houses, or, at least we make phone calls and sometime we may call them in small batches on the afternoon tea session, or, in the dinner on the holidays. And we should be particular in planning for attending their social functions like marriage, birthday, special worship in a house, when we are invited.

The fifth balance lies in the modality of expenditures. So far I was discussing about the human relations in closed groups right from the small family unit to the inner circle of the friends and relations. Now I discuss on the balance in the income and the expenditures under different planned and non-planned accounts of the house. The non-planned accounts are those which we cannot curtail, like the expenditures towards rental accommodation, school and college fees, optimum food items and groceries, electricity bill, cooking gas, optimum daily transport charges, doctor's fees and medicines (when required). The planned expenditures are those which could have been avoided or reduced, like the expenditures for personal habits and personal pleasures, entertainment for the family, excursions, purchase of branded items, expenditures towards show-off items, purchase of land or residential accommodation, keeping persons for cooking, housekeeping etc. Then we should also plan for saving some money for future. Unless we keep a balance between planned and non-planned expenditures, we are gone. We may be in uncalled for debt, bringing trouble for us. Cut your coat according to the cloth you have. This may be a chest coat, a full sleeve coat, a long coat. Keep a balance between temptation and need. We purchase a lot of things, place them in the house and then forget them. The dust goes on accumulating on them. The home space shrinks. Ultimately it becomes wastage of money.

There also comes the balance in our own body. The physical balance and the mental balance are dependent on each other. Too much physical stress would disorder the mental balance. And too much non-stop mental activity would have a bad effect on the physical balance, on the balance of the different organs of the body. To remain calm and clear headed, a balance is necessary between the physical and the mental activities. Anything overdone has a bad effect. We work to make the life better, but too much work to achieve a goal quickly derails the enjoyment from life. One day you will find that you have missed many things in your life, for which you are repenting now. There are people who even defer their marriage to give more time to achieve their goals. And a delayed marriage at the age of 40s and 50s puts them in a situation where they are under great mental pressure for bringing up the children properly.

And there also should be a plan to live for others, extending your helping hand for the needy. It may be a physical help, a mental help and/or a financial help. There should be the attitude of helping others. No matter, whether it is a big help or a small help. It should go as per your ability, but do it. It would give a pleasure to you, which cannot be purchased by any amount of money.

So, dear friends, do not spend the early life on whims. Have a proper plan to have sustained pleasure till you retire from the present life.

Let us stop here now. If Time permits, I would narrate my experiences in the deep interiors in the Democratic Republic of Congo in a separate book. You would feel that God is everywhere to save you, if you earnestly pray for it.

Have a good time.

Your Aged Friend
Samir

sarkar1942@hotmail.com